The Book of the Living Flame

44 Hermetic Laws

THE BOOK OF THE LIVING FLAME

44 Hermetic Laws

Transmitted Through

Ancient The Architect

© 2025 **Ancient the Architect**
All rights reserved.
Published by **Health Is Luxury LLC**

Cover design and interior artwork © 2025 by Ancient the Architect

No part of this publication may be reproduced, stored in a retrieval system, or transmitted in any form or by any means—electronic, mechanical, photocopying, recording, or otherwise—without the prior written permission of the copyright holder, except in the case of brief quotations embodied in critical articles or reviews.

This book is a work of metaphysical philosophy and spiritual reflection. It is intended for educational, meditative, and inspirational use. The author and publisher do not guarantee historical, scientific, psychological, or medical outcomes. Readers are encouraged to use discernment and personal insight when interpreting the material.

ISBN: 979-8-9922102-4-8

First Edition: 2025
Printed in the United States of America

Publisher:
Health Is Luxury LLC

TABLE OF CONTENTS

SECTION I: FOUNDATIONS OF THE DIVINE ARCHITECTURE

The Ground of the Flame (Laws 1–10)

   The Law of Divine Mind (Nous)
   The Law of Emanation
   The Law of Correspondence
   The Law of Motion and Return
   The Law of Spiritual Ascent (Rebirth)
   The Law of Silence and Mystery
   The Law of Light and Darkness
   The Law of the Heart as the Throne of the Soul
   The Law of the Logos (Divine Word)
   The Law of Unity

SECTION II: THE ASCENT OF THE SOUL

Lifting the Flame (Laws 11–20)

   The Law of the Great Chain of Being
   The Law of Becoming and Being
   The Law of the Soul's Weighing and Judgment
   The Law of Purification Through the Elements
   The Law of Harmony Through the Spheres
   The Law of the Living Cosmos
   The Law of Divine Imagination
   The Law of Ascent Through Contemplation

The Law of the Eighth Sphere
The Law of Sacred Union (Syzygy)

SECTION III: ALCHEMICAL AND COSMIC PRINCIPLES

Transmuting the Flame (Laws 21–30)

The Law of the Self-Created (Autogenesis)
The Law of Anagoge (The Upward Path)
The Law of the Generative Word (Logismos)
The Law of the Hidden Fire (Pneuma)
The Law of the Eternal Return
The Law of Divine Memory
The Law of the Unseen Hand (Providence and Necessity)
The Law of the Sacred Body (Temple of the Soul)
The Law of the Generative Light
The Law of Divine Silence (The Ineffable)

SECTION IV: APEX METAPHYSICS OF DIVINE RETURN

Becoming the Flame (Laws 31–44)

The Law of Divine Containment (The All in All)
The Law of Eternal Simultaneity (Time as Thought)
The Law of Recursive Creation (The Creator Creates the Creator)
The Law of Reversed Perception (The Descent is Ascent)
The Law of Harmonic Resonance (Tuning the Soul to the Real)
The Law of Sacred Density (The Wisdom of Embodied Light)

The Law of the Infinite Interior (Depth Over Distance)
The Law of Sacred Irreversibility (The Seal of Becoming)
The Law of Wordless Transfer (Transmission Through Being)
The Law of Veiled Clarity (Truth Hidden by Revelation)
The Law of Double Vision (Seeing the Real Behind the Real)
The Law of Silent Reversal (The Descent of the Divine Into You)
The Law of the Eternal Stranger (God as the Unknown Within)
The Law of Returnless Unity (The End That Has No Opposite)

ATLANTEAN SCROLLS APPENDIX

Prophetic Verses Re-rendered from the Emerald Tablets of Thoth

The Hidden Vessel Beneath the Guardian of Stone
The Flame Within and the Masters of Time
The Halls of the Hidden Scrolls
The Song of Vibration
The Keepers of the Threshold
The Dark Brothers Who Feed on Fear
The Halls of Amenti
The Lords of the Cycles
The Light That Burns in the Shadow
The Keys of Magic
The Path of the Serpent Fire
The Sun Behind the Sun
The Silence Before the Word
The Death That Is Not Death
My Departure and Return

Final Prophecy of Thoth

The Hidden Vessel Beneath the Guardian of Stone
(A retranslation of the complete Emerald Tablet passage with commentary)

Preface

To those who remember the flame...

This book is not meant to be read.
It is meant to be entered.

These 44 Hermetic Laws are not rules, nor teachings, nor beliefs.
They are **frequencies**—vibrational structures whispered from the deeper silence of the Divine Mind, encoded within the ancient Hermetica.

Each law is a door.
Each door is a mirror.
And what you see in the mirror will not be the world—but **yourself before time**.

These pages carry no doctrine, only direction.
No dogma, only disclosure.
They speak not to the intellect, but to the soul that has grown weary of forgetting.

What follows is not philosophy.
It is memory, encoded as fire.

You are not being taught.
You are being **reminded**.

Return to the flame.

— *The Architect, Scribe of the One Mind*

Opening Invocation

To Be Read in Silence Before the Scroll is Opened

O seeker of the inner light,
Who stands at the gate of the One Fire—
Let not your lips rush to speak,
Let not your mind rush to judge.

These are not teachings to be understood,
But thresholds to be crossed.

The voice you hear here is not a voice,
But a flame—a memory of God,
Burning in the ashes of your forgotten divinity.

This scroll is not for the world.
It is for the fire you lost,
And the Self you are becoming again.

In reverence, begin.
In silence, receive.
In becoming, return.

Introduction

On the Living Flame and the Laws That Return You to It

There is a light within you that has never gone out.
Not since your descent into form.
Not through sorrow or success.
Not even in your deepest forgetting.

The ancients called it the **Living Flame**—
the self-born fire at the center of the soul,
the reflection of the Divine that never fragmented,
the core of all things that was never created and will never end.

The Hermetica, attributed to **Thoth-Hermes Trismegistus**, is one of the rare transmissions that does not describe this flame, but **awakens it**. In poetic paradox and veiled speech, it reveals the secret path of the soul:

- its emanation from the One

- its descent into the world

- its sleep within matter

- and its ascent, not back, but **inward**, to become what it always was.

This book is the distillation of those revelations.

The **44 Laws** contained here are not laws in the modern sense. They are **structures of spiritual reality**, principles that govern not what you must do, but what **already is**. They are the invisible architecture of the cosmos, the soul, and the way home.

They are drawn from the **original Hermetic texts**—*Poimandres*, the *Corpus Hermeticum*, and the *Asclepius*. Each law has been extracted, clarified, and transcribed in the spirit of **purity, precision, and power**, for the modern seeker who has no time to waste on half-truths or empty mysticism.

There are no prayers in this book.
No affirmations.
No rituals.
Only the laws of the soul in its **eternal return** to what it has always been.

This book is the fire's memory.
May it ignite your own.

Law 1: The Law of Divine Mind (Nous)

Source: *Corpus Hermeticum I (Poimandres)*

At the foundation of Hermetic wisdom is the concept of the **Nous**, the Divine Mind, which is the **first emanation of the One (The All)**. Everything in creation originates from this intelligent, conscious source. It is through this Mind that all things were imagined, shaped, and brought into being.

Hermetic Insight

The Nous is male and female, light and life—**a unity of opposites**, containing within itself all possibilities. Through the Divine Mind, the Logos (Word) emerges, setting creation in motion.

> **"The Nous, which is God, being male and female, life and light, brought forth by His Word another Nous—the Creator of the world."**
> (*Poimandres, CH I*)

Implication

To understand creation, the soul must return to and commune with the Nous. The human mind, as a spark of this Divine Mind, has the potential to awaken to cosmic truth.

This law originates from the opening passages of *Poimandres*, the first and most foundational text in the Hermetica. In this sacred vision, Hermes experiences the revelation of the **Divine Mind (Nous)** as the original essence from which all things flow. He is told that Nous is **not just intelligence, but the living awareness of the All**—the source of light, order, soul, and cosmos. In this state, Hermes doesn't merely learn about Nous—he **becomes one with it**, and from that unity, the rest of creation is revealed.

This directly mirrors the **Kybalion's Principle of Mentalism**, which states:

"The All is Mind; the Universe is Mental."

The Hermetic Nous is the **living intelligence of the cosmos**, meaning that reality is not made of matter, but of **thought structured by divine will**. This sets the foundation for every law that follows: **all things exist within the mind of the All, and man, by ascending, may consciously return to it.**

LAW 2: THE LAW OF EMANATION

Source: *Corpus Hermeticum II, X*

Creation flows **not from nothing**, but through a radiant **outpouring of divine essence**. This process is known as *emanation*. The One (The All) gives rise to the Nous, the Logos, the soul, and eventually the material world, all as **gradual unfoldings** of its own infinite nature.

Unlike creation ex nihilo (out of nothing), Hermeticism teaches that everything that exists was always **within the One** and is now **unfolded outward**, like light streaming from a source.

Hermetic Insight

"From the One comes the All, and from the All returns to the One. All things are one, and come from the One."
(*Corpus Hermeticum X*)

"The Good is in nothing but itself. It is the cause of all things... not created, for all things are made by it."
(*CH II*)

Implication

You are not separate from the Divine Source—you are an emanation of it. Spiritual awakening means **tracing your own light back to its origin**. The higher you ascend in consciousness, the closer you come to your divine root.

This law emerges from *Corpus Hermeticum II*, where Hermes receives the teaching that creation is not an act of separation, but a process of **overflow**. The Divine, being full and infinite, does not create out of need or lack—it **emanates**. All things come forth from the One as **expressions of its inner fullness**, like rays from the sun or ripples from a centerless light. In this, Hermes is taught that the cosmos is not something made—but something continuously **born** from the inner nature of God.

This vision aligns with the **Kybalion's Principle of Vibration**, which states:

"Nothing rests; everything moves; everything vibrates."

Emanation is the first vibration—the motion of being from stillness, the descent of unity into multiplicity. The Law of Emanation shows that **you are not distant from Source—you are the echo of its first movement**.

LAW 3: THE LAW OF CORRESPONDENCE

Source: *Asclepius, Corpus Hermeticum XI*

This principle teaches that **everything in the universe is connected** through a web of reflective patterns. The macrocosm (the universe) and the microcosm (man) are **mirrors of each other**. What happens in the heavens is reflected on Earth; what happens within the soul is mirrored in the cosmos.

It's from this Hermetic insight that the axiom **"As above, so below"** was born—though that exact phrase is more famously seen on the **Emerald Tablet**, its spiritual and philosophical roots are **directly found in the Hermetica**.

Hermetic Insight

"Man is a marvel, O Asclepius. For he is connected with the gods above and with the beings below. He is not just a part of the world—he is like a god in the world."
(*Asclepius*)

"Understand this: you are in the image of the cosmos, and the cosmos is in the image of God."
(*Corpus Hermeticum XI*)

Implication

By understanding yourself, you understand the universe. When you elevate your inner world, your outer world changes to match. Everything is governed by sacred symmetry.

This law is illuminated in *Corpus Hermeticum XI*, where Hermes is taught that the universe is constructed in mirrored layers. Everything above has a reflection below, and nothing exists in isolation. The human being is described as a **microcosm**—a miniature of the great All—containing within himself the same divine order found in the stars, elements, and celestial spheres. The sacred task of the initiate is to recognize these inner correspondences and **use them as bridges** to ascend inwardly through self-knowledge.

This principle is explicitly mirrored in the **Kybalion's Principle of Correspondence**, which declares:

"As above, so below; as below, so above."

In the Hermetic worldview, this is more than metaphor—it is a **spiritual technology**. To truly understand the nature of any reality, the adept must look for its twin within. The law teaches that **what is seen is the echo of what is unseen**, and the key to unlocking heaven is hidden inside your very form.

LAW 4: THE LAW OF MOTION AND RETURN

Source: *Corpus Hermeticum XIII, Corpus Hermeticum I (Poimandres)*

All things are in **eternal motion**, and that motion follows a divine arc: **descent from the One and return to the One**. Nothing in the "Hermetic" universe is static. The soul, like all emanations, **descends into form**, experiences separation, and then **ascends back** through purification and gnosis.

This law reveals the sacred cycle: birth, manifestation, and spiritual return. Even the cosmos itself is part of this motion—expanding from unity and eventually being drawn back into it.

Hermetic Insight

"**The human soul is divine, and it returns to the divine. It suffers being in the body as a trial—but through gnosis and purification, it returns to its source.**"
(*Corpus Hermeticum XIII*)

"**The soul that is not impious departs the body and is received by the divine. It mounts upward through the spheres... and enters the region of the intelligible.**"
(*Poimandres, CH I*)

Implication

This law encourages spiritual seekers to not remain bound by material illusions. Your life is not a random event—it is a **path of return**, and you are meant to ascend again through remembrance of your divine origin.

This law unfolds most clearly in *Corpus Hermeticum IX*, where Hermes is shown that the cosmos is not inert matter, but a **living divine body**, ensouled by the intelligence of the One. The heavens, stars, and planetary spheres are not external phenomena—they are **conscious emanations** in a vast divine organism. The cosmos is referred to as a **god in motion**, a sacred body through which the will of the All is continuously expressed.

This structure reflects the **Kybalion's Principle of Correspondence** at a deeper esoteric octave—not merely "as above, so below," but:

As the Cosmos is a Body to God, so your body is a cosmos to the divine spark within you.

In this view, the Hermetic initiate recognizes that the heavens and the self are built on the **same metaphysical architecture**. The celestial spheres are not distant—they are **living organs of divine will**, and man is the inner image of that holy structure. To understand the heavens, one must listen to the divine echo **within the cellular temple of the body**.

LAW 5: THE LAW OF SPIRITUAL ASCENT (REBIRTH)

Source: *Corpus Hermeticum XIII, Poimandres (CH I)*

True rebirth is not of the body, but of the **spirit**. The Hermetica teaches that to ascend, the soul must undergo **inner regeneration**—a conscious rebirth into divine awareness. This is not symbolic: it is a metaphysical transformation where the soul sheds ignorance, purifies the passions, and awakens to its divine nature.

This rebirth is called *palingenesia*, the awakening into the higher self through the **death of the lower self**.

Hermetic Insight

"**My child, you are born again from the truth. You are reborn as a god, a son of the One. The birth of the divine is not of the body—it is of the heart and the Nous.**"
(*Corpus Hermeticum XIII*)

"**You cannot understand what is divine unless you become divine.**"
(*Poimandres, CH I*)

Implication

To ascend spiritually, you must **die to the illusions of the material world** and awaken to the divine image within you. Gnosis (inner knowing) is the midwife of rebirth.

Through this law, the human being transforms from a mortal into a participant in divine consciousness.

This law is unveiled in *Corpus Hermeticum XIII*, where Hermes initiates his son Tat into the mystery of **second birth**—not from flesh, but from **truth and fire**. Tat undergoes an inner transformation, in which he sheds his mortal identity and awakens to his divine nature. This rebirth is not metaphor—it is a metaphysical transition in which the soul reclaims its **original state before descent**, becoming pneuma (spirit) once more. The process is violent, ecstatic, and irreversible. One does not simply believe—they **become**.

This law correlates subtly with the **Kybalion's Principle of Rhythm**, but at an **occult octave**. Not the surface rhythm of polarity, but the **return rhythm of spirit**:

Everything flows in and out. All rise and fall. But the soul that remembers its source reverses the cycle.

In the Kybalionic system, rhythm governs return—but here, Hermes reveals that true rebirth breaks the cycle entirely. The one who undergoes spiritual ascent no longer swings between opposites—they are **lifted out of rhythm**, into stillness. The reborn soul does not escape life—it reenters life as **a luminous force**, no longer bound by polarity or fate.

6. The Law of Silence and Mystery

Source: *Corpus Hermeticum I (Poimandres), CH XI, CH XII*

Hermetic knowledge is not meant for all. The deepest truths are hidden within **sacred silence**, revealed only to the worthy through inner awakening and divine initiation. The Hermetica consistently warns against revealing divine mysteries to those who are not yet ready, emphasizing that **wisdom is guarded by mystery** and must be approached with reverence and purity.

The initiate is urged to remain silent—not only out of secrecy, but out of **spiritual protection** for the unready and as a sign of respect for the ineffable.

Hermetic Insight

"Keep silent, O my child. This discourse I have spoken to you is sacred, and it must be concealed. It is not permitted to speak of these things to those unworthy."
(*Corpus Hermeticum I*)

"This knowledge is not taught, it is found through the silence of the Nous. For what is divine cannot be spoken—it must be known in stillness."
(*CH XI*)

Implication

Spiritual truths cannot be fully captured in words—they are known through the heart, in stillness, through communion with the Divine Mind. This law invites you to **protect the sacred**, speak only when the soul is ready to hear, and honor the path of the initiate by walking in quiet wisdom.

This law emerges in *Corpus Hermeticum I* and *CH V*, where Hermes is taken beyond the boundary of spoken instruction and into a realm where the soul must **perceive truth without language**. In his initiatory vision, Hermes learns that the highest realities are not communicated by speech, but by presence. The Divine is said to be **ineffable** not because it is hidden, but because it is **too vast to be contained by form, symbol, or sound**. This silence is not emptiness—it is the fullness before all form. In that stillness, all knowing becomes one.

The sacred mysteries withdraw when forced into words. This law teaches that wisdom ripens not in expression, but in **interior stillness**, where the soul's flame comes into direct alignment with the unspeakable. The most powerful transmissions are not uttered, but encountered—between thought and breath, beyond image and echo.

LAW 7: THE LAW OF LIGHT AND DARKNESS

Source: *Poimandres (Corpus Hermeticum I), CH V, CH XI*

All of creation is a play between **Light and Darkness**, not as moral opposites, but as metaphysical conditions. **Light** is divine consciousness—truth, being, and illumination. **Darkness** is ignorance, separation, and illusion. The soul's journey is to pass from the shadows of matter into the radiance of divine light.

Darkness is not evil, but **the absence of gnosis (inner knowledge)**. The Hermetica speaks of the "dark mist" or "wet chaos" as the realm of confusion and forgetfulness from which the awakened soul must emerge.

Hermetic Insight

"I saw a great light, a joyful and boundless vision. And in it was a divine being. But I also saw a great darkness coiling downward—a chaos of shadow and watery nature. And I knew: that which rises is of the light, that which sinks is of ignorance."
(*Poimandres, CH I*)

"The soul that binds itself to body alone wanders in darkness. But the soul that opens to the light of Nous rises upward like a star."
(*CH V*)

Implication

Light is your true nature, but you must reclaim it through remembrance. The mind that clings to matter remains in the dark; the soul that turns to the divine is **illumined from within**. Every choice you make either deepens your shadow or expands your light.

This law is drawn from *Corpus Hermeticum V* and *CH I (Poimandres)*, where Hermes beholds a sacred polarity—not of good versus evil, but of **consciousness and potential**, expressed as light and darkness. In the beginning of his vision, he witnesses a primordial darkness—a watery abyss—and from it, a holy light emerges, filled with divine reason. Yet this light does not destroy the darkness; it **organizes it**. The Hermetic tradition affirms that darkness is not the enemy of light—it is its **womb**.

Light reveals, but it is darkness that **conceals the unformed**, holding all that might yet become. These two are not opposites in conflict, but **twin forces in creative tension**. The initiate does not flee darkness, but enters it with awareness, transforming shadow into understanding.

This law resonates with the **Kybalion's Principle of Polarity**, which teaches that extremes are the same in nature, differing only in degree. The Hermetica extends this idea: light and darkness are **not enemies**, but **degrees of realization** within the divine field. The adept who embraces both becomes whole—not divided between purity and fear, but integrated as a vessel of radiant wisdom born of both realms.

LAW 8: THE LAW OF THE HEART AS THE THRONE OF THE SOUL

Source: *Corpus Hermeticum IV, CH XII*

In Hermetic teaching, the **heart** is not merely an emotional center—it is the **throne of the soul**, the sacred chamber where divine truth is received and reflected. While the Nous (Divine Mind) is the source of illumination, it is the **purified heart** that becomes its vessel.

The soul cannot rise to the divine unless the heart is cleansed of ignorance, passion, and error. This purification allows the heart to become the **mirror of the divine**, where sacred wisdom is not taught but felt, known, and lived.

Hermetic Insight

"The soul resides in the heart, my child, and the heart must be made holy. For only then can it reflect the image of the Divine Nous."
(*Corpus Hermeticum IV*)

"Withdraw into yourself, and a divine temple shall be built in your heart. There the divine speaks, not in words, but in presence."
(*CH XII*)

Implication

This law teaches that wisdom is not merely intellectual—it must be **inscribed upon the heart**. To know the divine, you must purify your inner temple. The awakened heart becomes a throne where the soul communes with the All.

This law comes from *Corpus Hermeticum IV*, where Hermes reveals the heart not as an organ of emotion, but as the **sacred throne of divine presence**. In the vision, the heart is described as the **centerpoint** between the soul's higher faculties and its physical incarnation. It is the axis where spirit and matter meet, and thus the place where the divine **chooses to dwell**. The soul must purify itself so that this heart can become an **unshakable seat of divine wisdom**, guiding the entire being toward its highest purpose.

The law speaks not of the physical heart, but of the **spiritual heart**, which serves as the channel through which divine light flows, and the vehicle by which the soul returns to its Source. The **power of the heart** is that it contains both **love** and **intelligence**—qualities that, when purified, align the soul with divine will.

This principle resonates with the **Kybalion's Principle of Gender**, but in a refined manner. While the Kybalion speaks of gender as manifesting in all planes of existence, **the heart embodies the unification of opposites**—masculine and feminine energies, intellect and intuition, which when balanced within the heart, create a powerful and enlightened vessel for divine presence.

LAW 9: THE LAW OF THE LOGOS (DIVINE WORD)

Source: *Poimandres (CH I), Corpus Hermeticum VIII, CH X*

The **Logos** is the **Divine Word or Reason**, born from the Nous (Divine Mind), through which all things are created and maintained. It is the **living expression of thought**, the vibration that sets the cosmos into ordered motion. In Hermetic philosophy, the Logos is not just sound—it is the **active force of divine intelligence** shaping the visible and invisible worlds.

Every act of creation is a word spoken by the Divine. Likewise, the human being—made in the image of the All—also creates through thought and speech, participating in the same divine function.

Hermetic Insight

"The Word (Logos) came forth from the Light and stood beside the Nous. It was the craftsman of the world."
(*Poimandres, CH I*)

"Man is a speaker, like his Father. The Logos within him is the echo of the cosmic Word."
(*CH VIII*)

"The Logos is the bond that holds heaven and earth, the harmony of all things."
(*CH X*)

Implication

This law reveals that creation is the result of a **spoken vibration**—not in sound, but in **pure spiritual intent**. To align with the divine is to master your own word, thought, and intent. When you speak truth from a purified soul, you participate in divine creation.

This law is directly rooted in *Corpus Hermeticum VIII*, where Hermes learns that the **Word (Logos)** is not merely a tool of communication, but the **living expression** of the Divine Mind. The Logos is described as the **first breath of creation**, the **source and channel of divine intelligence** that holds the cosmos together. Hermes is shown that everything in the universe—its form, its order, its movement—stems from **the Divine Thought** expressed through the Word. It is the **shaper of reality** and the sacred **vibration** that underlies all matter and spirit.

This ties deeply with the **Kybalion's Principle of Cause and Effect**, but in a more subtle, spiritual way. The **Logos** represents the **first cause**—the **origin of all effects** in the manifested world. It reveals that every effect, whether material or metaphysical, can be traced back to a **first word**—a divine utterance of intent and will. The law teaches that when we align with the **Logos**, we align ourselves with the **divine cause** of all things, transcending the illusions of randomness or chance. The Word governs all laws of the cosmos, shaping them with deliberate divine intelligence.

LAW 10: THE LAW OF UNITY

Source: *Corpus Hermeticum II, CH XI, CH XII*

At the heart of Hermetic philosophy is the revelation that **all is One**. There is no true separation—only **appearance**. The Divine is not outside of creation, but within it, as its **substance, essence, and mind**. Every god, soul, star, and atom is a **mode of the One Being**, expressed in different forms and levels.

This is the foundational metaphysical law: **Unity precedes all multiplicity**. To awaken is to remember that every division is illusion, and that **you are not separate from the cosmos—you are the cosmos, aware of itself**.

Hermetic Insight

"All things are one, and the One is all things. For all things were in the Creator before being created."
(*Corpus Hermeticum II*)

"There is One Light, One Mind, One Life flowing through all. The wise know this unity, and from it draw peace."
(*CH XI*)

"Do not say God is in heaven, or in the sea, or on the earth. God is All. There is nothing that is not God."
(*CH XII*)

Implication

This law dissolves all fear, all ego, and all illusion. The realization of Unity is the goal of all Hermetic practice. The further you move toward this truth, the more you **become the All, while still being yourself**. This is not the loss of individuality, but the fulfillment of your divine identity.

This law emerges from *Corpus Hermeticum II*, where Hermes is shown that **the One** is not a distant principle but the **origin of all that is**. The cosmos, in its myriad forms, arises from a singular source, and all things in existence are **expressions of this undivided unity**. Hermes receives the revelation that the concept of separation is an illusion: **there is no 'other,' no duality**—everything is **contained within the One**. The soul's ultimate return is not to a place or a state, but to the realization of this **unbroken oneness**.

This law deeply resonates with the **Kybalion's Principle of Polarity**, but at a more profound level. While the Kybalion speaks of opposites and duality being extremes of the same essence, the Hermetic teaching here goes beyond mere polarity. It teaches that **all dualities are aspects of a singular whole**, and even the apparent opposites—light and dark, good and evil, spirit and matter—are but **manifestations of the One**. True enlightenment is the **realization** that the soul has never been separate from the divine unity, but simply **unaware** of its inherent oneness.

LAW 11: THE LAW OF THE GREAT CHAIN OF BEING

Source: *Asclepius, Corpus Hermeticum XI, CH IX*

All existence is arranged in a **hierarchical chain**, descending from the Divine Source to matter. This is known as the **Great Chain of Being**—a continuous spectrum of life, intelligence, and consciousness stretching from the highest gods to the densest minerals.

Each level of being is **interconnected** and flows into the next:

God → **Mind (Nous)** → Soul → Stars → Spirits → Humans → Animals → Plants → Stones

Man occupies a **unique midpoint**, bridging heaven and earth. This makes the human being a **microcosm**, holding within him all the levels of creation and capable of rising or falling through the chain.

Hermetic Insight

"**In man is mingled the nature of the divine and of the mortal. He is linked to the gods above and to the beings below.**"

(*Asclepius*)

"The cosmos is a living being; the stars are gods; the earth is filled with spirits, animals, and forms. And man is born of them all."
(*Corpus Hermeticum IX*)

"Everything is full of soul, and all is bound in one harmony."
(*CH XI*)

Implication

This law reveals your **sacred position**: you are not merely human—you are the **intermediary between realms**. Your choices either elevate you up the chain (toward divinity) or drag you downward into density. Mastery lies in harmonizing your being with the entire chain.

This law comes from *Corpus Hermeticum XI*, where Hermes describes the **universal order of existence** as a **Great Chain** that connects all things, from the most divine to the most material. Each being, whether an angel, a planet, an animal, or a stone, exists in a precise **hierarchical order**, with each part of creation vibrating at its own frequency, yet all **interconnected** through a divine web. Hermes reveals that no part of creation is ever truly separate, for each link in the chain is both **unique** and **necessary** to the whole. This principle teaches that the universe is not random but **perfectly ordered**, with each being fulfilling its specific role in the divine plan.

This law correlates deeply with the **Kybalion's Principle of Correspondence**, but it extends the principle beyond individual correspondence. The **Great Chain of Being** is the **cosmic embodiment of correspondence** in its highest form. As Hermes teaches, the "above" exists within the "below," but this law clarifies that **the above also permeates the below**—as **divinity** flows through all planes, and each level of existence is a mirror of the divine order.

LAW 12: THE LAW OF BECOMING AND BEING

Source: *Corpus Hermeticum XI, CH VIII, CH X*

In the Hermetica, a clear distinction is made between **Being** (the eternal, unchanging divine essence) and **Becoming** (the realm of time, change, and manifestation). All visible things exist in a state of *becoming*—they are born, grow, decay, and die. But behind this flux lies **Being**, the unchanging source of all that is.

Everything that comes to be does so through motion and transformation, but only **that which is eternal and immovable** truly *is*. The goal of the initiate is to rise from the illusions of becoming into the realization of **true Being**.

Hermetic Insight

"That which is born is always changing and becoming, but that which is unbegotten neither comes into being nor changes. It simply is."
(*Corpus Hermeticum XI*)

"All that becomes is under the law of time, but Being is above it, eternal and perfect."
(*CH X*)

"O Soul, why do you love what becomes, and not what is? Seek the eternal, and you shall be free."
(*CH VIII*)

Implication

You live in a world of constant becoming, but your true essence belongs to **Being**—the divine, unchanging reality. The path of Hermetic mastery is to awaken to that which is **eternal within you**, and to recognize all passing forms as reflections, not reality.

This law originates from *Corpus Hermeticum XI, CH VIII, and CH X*, where Hermes reveals the deep mystery of **becoming** and **being**. The Hermetica teaches that the process of **becoming** is not a movement toward something **other** but a return to the original state of **being**. The soul, in its journey through matter, experiences a **veil of forgetfulness**, which causes it to believe in the illusion of its separateness. In truth, the soul is **always already divine**—it is simply in the process of **remembering** its true nature.

Hermes instructs that **being** is not something the soul acquires—it is something the soul **recovers**. The state of being divine is the **eternal truth**; becoming is simply the soul's **realignment** with this truth.

This law is deeply connected with the **Kybalion's Principle of Vibration**. While the Kybalion emphasizes the continual movement and transformation of everything, **the Law of Becoming and Being** shows that this movement is not aimless. It is a rhythm of **remembering**—a vibration of **the soul's return to its original state of divine presence**. Through purification, the soul sheds the layers of illusion and **vibrates at the frequency of divine being**, thereby returning to the unity of the All.

LAW 13: THE LAW OF THE SOUL'S WEIGHING AND JUDGMENT

Source: *Corpus Hermeticum I (Poimandres), CH XIII,* **Egyptian Book of the Dead (parallel teaching)**

Upon death—or the death of ignorance during spiritual awakening—the soul undergoes a **metaphysical weighing**. This is not judgment by an external god, but by the **soul's own nature**, which rises or falls based on its alignment with truth, purity, and the divine order.

In the Hermetica, this is described as the soul ascending through the **seven planetary spheres**, each stripping away lower attachments (such as lust, pride, greed, etc.) until only the pure essence remains. If the soul is weighed down by ignorance, it is drawn back into rebirth; if light and pure, it ascends to the divine.

This concept mirrors the ancient Egyptian ritual of the **Weighing of the Heart**, where the heart was placed on scales against the feather of Ma'at (truth, balance).

Hermetic Insight

"Each soul, when released from the body, passes through the spheres. At each, it surrenders that which does not belong to it, until it becomes pure spirit and enters the Eighth Sphere."
(*Poimandres, CH I*)

"The soul is judged not by decree, but by its own nature. The impure are drawn downward; the pure rise to the divine."
(*CH XIII*)

Implication

This law teaches that **the state of your soul is the final judge**. What you carry within—your desires, fears, virtues, and attachments—determines whether you rise or return. The purification of the soul is not for the afterlife alone—it is the central task of this life.

This law is drawn from *Corpus Hermeticum I (Poimandres), CH XIII*, where Hermes describes the soul's ascent after death and its **weighing** in the divine balance. The soul is judged by **Ma'at**, the ancient Egyptian principle of divine truth, justice, and order. In this vision, the soul is not judged by mere external actions but by its **alignment with the truth**—how it has lived in accordance with universal harmony and **divine law**. The weighing process does not simply assess deeds but the **balance of the heart and mind, one's true intent**, which must align with Ma'at's divine order.

The law reveals that true judgment is not an arbitrary decision, but a reflection of the soul's **inner harmony with the eternal laws of the universe**. In the Hermetic tradition, this **inner balance** is what allows the soul to pass into higher realms or remain bound by the consequences of its disharmony. The divine judgment is not punishment, but

revelation, where the soul comes to understand the true **cost of its thoughts, actions, and intentions**.

This law profoundly resonates with the **Kybalion's Principle of Cause and Effect**, as it affirms that every action, thought, and intention reverberates throughout the cosmos, contributing to the **soul's journey**. In Ma'at's judgment, the effects of those vibrations are fully realized, and only when the soul aligns with the **universal law of truth and justice** can it ascend. This judgment is an **unfolding of the soul's relationship with cosmic order**, revealing where it has strayed and where it has stayed true.

LAW 14: THE LAW OF PURIFICATION THROUGH THE ELEMENTS

Source: *Corpus Hermeticum XIII, CH X, CH V*

The Hermetica teaches that the soul, in its descent into materiality, becomes enmeshed with the **four lower elements**—earth, water, air, and fire. Each element corresponds to layers of the self: body, emotion, thought, and desire. To rise back to the divine, the soul must undergo **purification through these elemental layers**.

Purification is both inward and cosmic. Through conscious spiritual practice—detachment, discipline, gnosis—the initiate **burns away the dross**, clarifies the waters, stills the winds of thought, and lifts the soul from the heaviness of earth.

This elemental transmutation is the very meaning of **alchemy** in Hermetic practice—not turning metals into gold, but turning the impure human into a **living divinity**.

Hermetic Insight

"You must strip off the garments of the elements. The body is of earth, the passions of water, the illusions of air, and the burning desire of fire. Cast them off, and rise naked into the light."
(*Corpus Hermeticum XIII*)

"The fire of the soul must be made pure; the air of the mind must be made still. Then the Word will speak within you."
(CH V)

"When the soul has cleansed itself of elemental confusion, it becomes a god among men."
(CH X)

Implication

This law reveals that liberation is not escape, but **transformation**. You must not deny the elements, but **purify your relationship to them**. The more aligned your soul becomes with the higher element—the quintessence, or spirit—the more you awaken to your eternal self.

This law is drawn from *Corpus Hermeticum XIII, CH X, CH V*, where Hermes imparts the sacred knowledge of **purification through the four classical elements**—earth, water, air, and fire. In this Hermetic teaching, the soul is not merely subjected to external purification, but must **actively purify itself through inner alignment with the primal elements**. Each element represents a **fundamental principle** that the soul must internalize and harmonize with in order to ascend. The **earth** represents stability and the material body, the **water** represents emotions and unconscious states, the **air** represents the intellect and thoughts, and **fire** represents the **spirit** or divine essence.

The law teaches that each of these elements contains within it both the **potential for entrapment** (when misaligned) and the **potential for transcendence** (when purified). For the soul to ascend to higher realms, it must **purify each element within itself**, shedding attachments to materiality, cleansing emotions of confusion, balancing intellectual pursuits, and allowing the divine spark to reign over the lower nature.

This law resonates profoundly with the **Kybalion's Principle of Rhythm**, which describes the **cyclical nature of existence**—the ebb and flow between opposing states. Just as the soul passes through rhythms of **lower and higher states**, so too does it encounter the rhythm of purification. **Purification through the elements** is the soul's ability to **return from the lower states to its higher essence** through the rhythmic transmutation of matter, emotion, thought, and spirit. Each element in its purest form represents a **vibration of divine essence**—and purification is the process of aligning each element with this divine state.

LAW 15: THE LAW OF HARMONY THROUGH THE SPHERES

Source: *Corpus Hermeticum I (Poimandres), CH X, CH XII*

The cosmos is not chaotic—it is governed by **divine harmony**. Each planet, star, and heavenly sphere emits a unique vibration, and together they form the **music of the spheres**—a silent, spiritual symphony of perfect order.

Man, as a microcosm of the universe, also contains these harmonics. When the soul is **aligned with the celestial order**, it experiences peace, power, and gnosis. When out of harmony, the soul is agitated, fragmented, and bound to fate.

This law teaches that true mastery is not force, but **resonance**—bringing your soul into alignment with the rhythm of the divine cosmos.

Hermetic Insight

"The spheres of heaven are governed by harmony. Each has its place, each its tone. Together they move in sacred order, singing the praises of the One."
(*Poimandres, CH I*)

"He who aligns with the harmony of the heavens moves with them and becomes like them. He who rebels against them is crushed by their motion."
(*CH XII*)

"Heaven's order is the order of the soul. What you hear inwardly is the echo of the stars."
(*CH X*)

Implication

You are not separate from the cosmos—you are a note in its eternal song. When you purify the soul and silence the distractions of the world, you begin to **hear the divine harmony**, and your life becomes a reflection of celestial balance. To live in harmony is to live in divine truth.

This law originates from *Corpus Hermeticum I (Poimandres), CH X, CH XII*, where Hermes teaches that the cosmos is **structured as a harmonious whole**, composed of interconnected **spheres** that resonate with one another. These spheres—whether physical, mental, or spiritual—are not isolated, but exist in a **sacred symphony**. Each sphere vibrates at a specific frequency, and the entire universe **exists through their unified harmonic resonance**. Hermes shows that all things, from the celestial bodies to the soul of man, are **woven together by the same divine music**.

The law teaches that **the soul must tune itself** to the cosmic harmony in order to ascend. Just as a musician tunes their instrument to the proper pitch, so too must the soul **realign** with the divine harmony that permeates all of creation. Only through this **alignment** can the soul rise above the discord of the material world and experience union with the divine order.

This law resonates with the **Kybalion's Principle of Vibration**, but with a more subtle and profound insight. The Principle of Vibration explains that everything in the universe is in constant motion and vibrates at its own frequency, but **the Law of Harmony Through the Spheres** goes further, showing that these vibrations are not random—they are **divinely orchestrated**. The cosmos itself is a **divine symphony**, and each soul, as it aligns with the higher spheres, must **find its place within this universal music**. **Harmony is not a mere balance of forces**, but the **divine alignment of all things** within the grand cosmic design.

LAW 16: THE LAW OF THE LIVING COSMOS

Source: *Corpus Hermeticum IX, CH X, Asclepius*

The Hermetica teaches that the universe is not a machine—it is a **living being**, animated by divine soul and filled with intelligence. Every part of it—stars, planets, elements, animals, and humans—are **organs in the body of the cosmos**. Nothing is dead or inanimate; all things live, move, and breathe by the power of divine life.

This law proclaims the **ensoulment of all nature**. Even what we call "matter" is infused with life-force. The trees, rivers, winds, and stones are all expressions of the One Life. Therefore, the cosmos is not to be exploited or feared, but revered as **the sacred body of God**.

Hermetic Insight

"The world is a living creature, my child, with a soul and a mind. It is full of life and divine breath."
(*Corpus Hermeticum IX*)

"There is nothing in the cosmos that is dead. All things are full of life—whether they speak or are silent."
(*CH X*)

"The Earth, the stars, the animals, and mankind are limbs of the same body. To harm one is to harm the whole."
(*Asclepius*)

Implication

This law restores sacredness to all existence. You walk not on dead ground, but within a **living divine being**. The more you perceive this life in all things, the more alive you become. Reverence, communion, and harmony with the living cosmos is the path of the Hermetic initiate.

This law is drawn from *Corpus Hermeticum IX, CH X* and *Asclepius*, where Hermes teaches that the cosmos is not a mechanical structure, but a **living, divine organism**. In this vision, Hermes perceives the entire universe as **ensouled**—imbued with intelligence, consciousness, and purpose. The heavens, the earth, and all things within it are **conscious expressions of the Divine Will**. The stars are not simply celestial bodies, but **divine beings**—conscious manifestations of divine intelligence. The cosmos, as a living entity, has a **mind** and a **soul** that permeates every particle, every element, every atom. It breathes, thinks, and moves with divine intention.

Hermes reveals that this living cosmos is **governed by a single, unifying intelligence**—the Divine Mind (Nous)—but it is not a passive mind. The **living cosmos** is in **constant interaction** with the souls of all beings. It listens, responds, and mirrors back the thoughts and actions of those who inhabit it. The idea that the universe is alive with divine intelligence shows that the **spiritual and material** realms are intertwined, not separate. Every atom, every life form, and every moment in time **contains the breath of the Divine**.

This law is connected with the **Kybalion's Principle of Rhythm**, but it goes beyond simple movement or flow. The **Rhythm** that governs the cosmos is not just cyclical; it is a **living rhythm**, a **pulse of life**, continuously guided by divine intelligence. The **cosmos itself is an ongoing, living process**, constantly shifting, evolving, and breathing in divine harmony. To recognize this law is to acknowledge that **the entire universe is a sacred being**, and the soul, in its journey, is never separate from this living, divine organism.

LAW 17: THE LAW OF DIVINE IMAGINATION

Source: *Corpus Hermeticum XI, CH XIII, CH V*

In Hermetic philosophy, **Imagination** is not fantasy—it is **a divine faculty**, the eye of the soul through which it perceives, shapes, and ascends to higher realities. Imagination is the inner mirror of the Nous (Divine Mind), and through it, the soul can grasp truths beyond the senses, commune with the gods, and even participate in creation.

The Hermetica often speaks in symbolic language because it is **imagination—not logic—that bridges the human with the divine**. This sacred faculty must be purified and awakened, for it is the very gateway to gnosis.

Hermetic Insight

"He who cultivates his inner vision shall see the truth of things. For God is not seen with the eyes, but with the imagination of the heart."
(*Corpus Hermeticum XI*)

"Imagine the divine form within you, and you shall become it. For the soul becomes what it contemplates."
(*CH XIII*)

"The Nous works through imagination—it shapes, it lifts, it transmits divine patterns into the soul."
(*CH V*)

Implication

This law calls you to reclaim your imagination as a **sacred tool**, not a distraction. When purified by truth and inward stillness, your imagination becomes a channel for higher vision and divine transformation. In the Hermetic path, **to imagine divinely is to become divine**.

This law is drawn from *Corpus Hermeticum XI, CH XIII, CH V*, where Hermes reveals that **Divine Imagination** is the true **creative force** of the universe. It is not mere thought or abstract mental activity, but the **divine power that shapes reality**. In this Hermetic vision, imagination is not the **product of the human mind**, but the **living essence of the Divine Mind** itself, which continuously manifests and creates all things. The **cosmos itself is a creation of imagination**—a living, breathing projection of divine thought.

Hermes teaches that human imagination is a reflection of the **Divine Imagination**. It is through the power of the imagination that the soul **reconnects with its divine origin** and begins to consciously align with the **higher mind** of the Divine. The soul's ability to imagine with clarity and purpose allows it to shape its reality, **transmute its experiences**, and elevate its state of being. The creative **act of imagining** is not merely fanciful or illusory—it is a

divine tool for transformation, leading the soul closer to divine unity.

This law echoes the **Kybalion's Principle of Gender**, which emphasizes the **balance of masculine and feminine energies**. In this context, **Divine Imagination** represents the **feminine principle of creation**—the receptive and nurturing force that shapes form from formlessness. The soul, through imagination, must align with the **universal creative principle** in order to co-create with the Divine, **bringing forth new realities from the pure potential of the void**. The law teaches that imagination is **not just creative power** but a **sacred act of divine cooperation**, through which the soul shapes the world in alignment with its higher, divine purpose.

LAW 18: THE LAW OF ASCENT THROUGH CONTEMPLATION

Source: *Corpus Hermeticum X, CH I (Poimandres), CH V*

The soul does not ascend through force or dogma—it rises through **contemplation**, which is the focused turning of the mind toward the divine. In Hermeticism, contemplation (*theoria*) is not passive reflection—it is **active union** with higher realities through deep inner stillness and devotion to truth.

By contemplating divine things, the soul becomes attuned to them. This inner gaze allows the soul to shed the lower forms and merge with the higher. **The more you contemplate the divine, the more you become like it.**

Hermetic Insight

"Contemplate the divine, and you will become divine. For the soul becomes what it gazes upon with love and truth."
(*Corpus Hermeticum X*)

"Cease from the senses, O Soul, and ascend inwardly. Let your mind contemplate what is eternal, and your wings shall grow."
(*CH V*)

"In silent vision, the soul rises through the spheres. It leaves the world and draws near to the Father."
(*Poimandres, CH I*)

Implication

This law teaches that your **inner attention is the stairway to heaven**. Whatever you contemplate, you magnetize and merge with. If you contemplate the body, you become mortal. If you contemplate truth, you become eternal. In this, contemplation is not thought—it is **divine vision from the soul's center**.

This law is drawn from *Corpus Hermeticum X, CH I (Poimandres), CH V*, where Hermes imparts the secret of **spiritual ascent** through the practice of **contemplation**. In this vision, Hermes is taught that the **path of spiritual elevation** is not through external acts or rituals but through the **inner act of contemplation**. The soul, in its journey, must withdraw from the distractions of the material world and focus inward, where it can **commune with the Divine Mind**. Contemplation is the **pure act of turning inward, focusing the heart and mind** on the divine principles that lie beyond appearance and illusion.

The law reveals that **ascent through contemplation** requires the soul to **let go of egoic desires** and the pull of the physical world. Only in silence and stillness can the soul **rise above the illusion of separation** and return to its divine source. This ascent is not immediate; it requires **practice, patience, and persistence**. The soul must persist in the discipline of focusing on the higher truth, gradually lifting itself into alignment with the divine **wisdom of the cosmos**.

This law also ties deeply with the **Kybalion's Principle of Vibration**, but in a more **esoteric** way. While the Kybalion describes all things as vibrating at their own frequency, the **Law of Ascent Through Contemplation** shows that the soul, through focused spiritual practice, can **raise its own vibrational frequency**. The soul aligns itself with the **higher vibrations** of divine consciousness through the **practice of inner stillness**—allowing it to connect with the **pure essence of the Divine Mind**. Contemplation, then, is the art of tuning one's being to the **divine rhythm** of the universe, which leads the soul on its **path of return** to divine union.

LAW 19: THE LAW OF THE EIGHTH SPHERE

Source: *Corpus Hermeticum I (Poimandres), CH XIII, CH X*

The Hermetica describes seven planetary spheres, each corresponding to lower forces, passions, and attachments. As the soul ascends, it sheds one quality at each sphere. Beyond the seventh lies the **Eighth Sphere**—the realm of the stars, the divine, the immortal. It is the **threshold of cosmic unity**, where the purified soul is freed from fate and reborn into divine identity.

This is not a place, but a **state of being**—transcendent, eternal, and radiant. Only the soul that has fully purified itself through gnosis, virtue, and contemplation may enter.

Hermetic Insight

"When the soul leaves the body, it rises through the seven spheres, giving back to each the powers it took. Freed from all, it enters the Ogdoad—the Eighth Sphere—and sings praises with the divine."
(*Poimandres, CH I*)

"Beyond the firmament lies the region of the fixed stars, the Eighth Heaven. There the soul becomes god, for it has returned to its source."
(*CH XIII*)

"To enter the Eighth is to leave behind fate and time. There, the soul is no longer man, but light."
(*CH X*)

The Seven Planetary Spheres

As described in **Corpus Hermeticum I: Poimandres, the Shepherd of Men**

"The soul ascends through the seven circles, giving back to each the qualities it took from them."

This is the text where Hermes undergoes a vision of the soul's descent into matter and **its return upward** through the planetary spheres. As the soul ascends, it *surrenders* qualities/attachments it had accumulated in embodiment. These passions are listed in order, and traditionally correspond to the seven classical planets in Hermetic cosmology.

Sphere 1 – Saturn

Attachment Shed: **Deceit**

- Falsehood, manipulation, distortion of truth
- The soul surrenders its tendency to mask its nature or operate with hidden motives

Sphere 2 – Jupiter

Attachment Shed: Arrogance

- Pride, superiority, false nobility
- The soul lets go of its sense of entitlement, hierarchy, and spiritual ego

Sphere 3 – Mars

Attachment Shed: Rage

- Violence, vengeance, domination
- The soul releases all attachment to destruction, force, and control through aggression

Sphere 4 – Sun

Attachment Shed: Ambition

- Hunger for fame, self-glorification, and worldly success
- Even spiritual ambition is relinquished; the soul ceases striving to "become great"

Sphere 5 – Venus

Attachment Shed: Lust

- Sensual craving, physical desire, emotional entanglement
- The soul transcends identification with beauty and longing for gratification

Sphere 6 – Mercury

Attachment Shed: Greed

- Possessiveness, accumulation of wealth or knowledge for power
- The soul releases acquisitiveness in all its forms—material or mental

Sphere 7 – Moon

Attachment Shed: Falsehood in the Heart / Illusion

- Emotional confusion, projection, sentimentality, illusion of separateness
- The soul surrenders its final self-image and prepares to enter pure being

Beyond the Spheres: The Eighth Region – The Ogdoad

- Once these seven burdens are surrendered, the soul passes into the **Ogdoadic Sphere**, beyond fate, time, and polarity.

- This realm corresponds to the **fixed stars**, and marks the beginning of **divine immortality**.

- There, the soul is **no longer a soul—but a god among gods**, participating consciously in the **Mind of the All**.

Implication

This law reveals the true aim of Hermetic initiation: not moral improvement, but **spiritual transfiguration**. To rise to the Eighth Sphere is to become one with the divine pattern of creation—to **return not as who you were, but as what you truly are**.

This law is drawn from *Corpus Hermeticum I (Poimandres), CH XIII, CH X*, where Hermes is shown a profound vision of the soul's journey through the **seven planetary spheres**, each corresponding to attachments, passions, and false identities that the soul must shed. Once the soul relinquishes the final illusion at the seventh sphere, it enters the **eighth sphere**—the realm of the **fixed stars**, also known in Hermetic tradition as the **Ogdoad**.

This sphere lies beyond the cycles of generation and corruption, beyond the grasp of fate and the polarity of opposites. In *Poimandres*, it is revealed as the region of **pure being**—a state in which the soul is no longer bound to reincarnation or to the lower worlds. It is not a place, but a **vibrational state of divine permanence**. The soul that reaches the eighth sphere has transcended mortality and has entered into **eternal communion with the Divine Mind**. There, the soul becomes a **god among gods**, conscious of its origin, nature, and function within the all-encompassing reality.

This law offers a deeper glimpse into the **true goal of Hermetic transformation**. It does not end with moral purification or intellectual understanding—it culminates in **divine reintegration**. The eighth sphere is not merely a realm to be entered; it is a state to be **embodied**. The initiate must, in life, begin to live as one who belongs to the eighth sphere—detached from illusion, clear in perception, and radiant in divine essence.

The passage through the spheres represents more than stages of ascent—it symbolizes the **alchemical stripping of identity**, until only the essence remains. In this way, the eighth sphere becomes the **rebirth of the soul into immortality**, and the full awakening of its eternal nature.

LAW 20: THE LAW OF SACRED UNION (SYZYGY)

Source: *Corpus Hermeticum XIII, CH V, CH II*

In the Hermetic tradition, the soul's liberation occurs through a **sacred union**—a mystical marriage between the lower soul (psyche) and the higher spirit (Nous or Logos). This union, often symbolized as **male and female, earth and heaven, or mind and heart**, is called *syzygy*, meaning "sacred pairing" or divine conjunction.

True spiritual awakening is not separation from the world, but the **inner harmonization of opposites**—where the divine masculine and feminine, the human and the divine, the active and the receptive—merge in wholeness. Through this union, the soul is no longer divided and is **reborn in divine likeness**.

Hermetic Insight

"You have become both male and female, both light and darkness, both mortal and immortal. You are all things at once, for you have become divine."
(*Corpus Hermeticum XIII*)

"Join the knowing mind to the receptive soul, and they shall produce divine offspring—truth and immortality."
(*CH V*)

> "God is all pairs in union: Father and Mother, Life and Light, Nous and Logos."
> (*CH II*)

Implication

This law teaches that the soul is perfected not by denial, but by **integration**. When the divine masculine and feminine energies unite within you, you become a living temple of harmony. This union is the key to divine power, gnosis, and immortality—it is **the inner alchemy of the gods**.

This law is drawn from *Corpus Hermeticum XIII, CH V, CH II*, where Hermes reveals the mystery of **Syzygy**—a sacred union of opposites. In the Hermetic teachings, Syzygy is not simply the merging of masculine and feminine principles, but the **unification of dual forces** within the soul and cosmos: spirit and matter, reason and intuition, light and darkness. In *CH XIII*, Hermes guides his disciple through the transformational process by which the **soul becomes androgynous—not in body, but in nature**. This is the sacred reintegration of the divided self, where all inner polarity dissolves into divine wholeness.

In *CH II*, this sacred union is revealed as the divine blueprint behind all creation. Every motion, every emanation, is born of **the pairing of opposites**, producing life, intelligence, and movement. Yet sacred union is not merely procreative—it is **alchemical**. It is the fusion of qualities within the soul that were once fragmented, returning to their **original undivided essence**. This Syzygy is not static—it is a **living alignment with the divine pattern**, restoring the soul to its primordial harmony.

This law illuminates the profound spiritual truth that **the human being is a mirror of cosmic balance**, and that true ascension requires the **soul's inner elements to marry in divine proportion**. When thought and feeling, will and surrender, light and shadow are brought into union, the soul becomes **a vessel of divine completeness**. It is this sacred inner marriage that prepares the soul to embody the higher mysteries and reflect the eternal image of the One.

LAW 21: THE LAW OF THE SELF-CREATED (AUTOGENESIS)

Source: *Corpus Hermeticum I (Poimandres), CH XI, CH XIII*

One of the most profound Hermetic teachings is that the divine is not simply a creator—it is **Self-Created**, or *Autogenes*. This means that **God is both cause and effect**, both the origin and what arises. Likewise, within man lies the **seed of autogenesis**—the power to consciously recreate oneself, to become not what the world made, but what the soul chooses to become.

This law reveals that spiritual rebirth is not given from without—it is **generated from within**. The divine spark in man, once awakened, becomes a **self-generating flame**—capable of ascending, illuminating, and renewing itself eternally.

Hermetic Insight

"The One who creates is Himself uncreated—He is Autogenes, the Self-Begotten, the Eternal Source. All things arise from Him, and He arises from none."
(*Poimandres, CH I*)

"The mind of man, once awakened, becomes a creator. He shapes his own being and is reborn not from flesh, but from spirit."
(*CH XIII*)

> "**You have been given power, my child, to generate yourself anew—to become a god from a man.**"
> (CH XI)

Implication

You are not a fixed being. You are a **living fire**, capable of rebirth, reinvention, and self-divinization. The power of *Autogenesis* is the power to **step outside of fate** and consciously choose your form, your path, and your light. To become divine is not to be saved—it is to **generate your own divine nature** from the inner source.

This law is drawn from *Corpus Hermeticum I (Poimandres)*, CH XI, CH XIII, where Hermes is shown the mystery of the **Self-Created**, known as **Autogenes**—the being who emerges not by birth through another, but through direct emanation from the Divine Mind. In *Poimandres*, this archetype is described as the **First Intellect**, born of Light and Mind, shining with its own essence and self-generated power. This Autogenes becomes the model not only for the macrocosm, but for the soul's true identity: **a being capable of self-generation through divine remembrance**.

In *CH XI*, Hermes receives a deeper initiation: he is taught that the perfected soul becomes like the Autogenes—it **becomes its own cause**, rising above fate, external influence, and even time. The true human being is not merely created but is called to **participate in creation**, to generate from within, to **speak reality into form** by the will of the divine spark. To reach this state, the initiate must purify all external dependencies and false identities, until only the **inner self-light remains**.

This law teaches that the soul is not meant to remain a passive creation but is destined to become a **co-creator**, capable of shaping destiny from within. The Autogenes is not simply a figure from divine history—it is a **living potential** within every soul. To realize it is to **stand in one's own divine fire**, no longer shaped by circumstance, but arising in full awareness of one's eternal nature and self-begotten power.

LAW 22: THE LAW OF ANAGOGE (THE UPWARD PATH)

Source: *Corpus Hermeticum XIII, CH I (Poimandres), CH IV*

Anagoge means "leading upward"—a mystical ascent of the soul through stages of awareness, shedding layers of illusion and matter, and climbing back toward its divine source. This law reveals that the soul's journey is not random, but follows a **spiral path of ascent**—from ignorance to knowledge, from form to essence, from separation to unity.

Each step upward requires **purification, understanding, and alignment**. The path winds through the planetary spheres, through the gates of inner transmutation, until the soul reaches the Eighth Sphere and beyond.

Hermetic Insight

"Rise, O soul, above your body, above the world, above the heavens. Cast off all that is not you, and ascend to that which is your source."
(*Corpus Hermeticum XIII*)

"The path upward is the path inward. As you ascend, you shall find yourself not in the sky, but in the center of the divine."
(*CH IV*)

> **"Seven guards stand at the gates of heaven, each stripping away an illusion. Only the naked soul may pass into eternity."**
> (*Poimandres, CH I*)

Implication

This law affirms that the **return to the divine is a structured path**, not a vague hope. You rise through conscious evolution. Every insight, every sacrifice, every moment of inner stillness moves you upward. The Hermetic journey is not one of escape—but of sacred ascent, step by step, back into the arms of the All.

This law is drawn from *Corpus Hermeticum XIII, CH I (Poimandres), and CH IV*, where Hermes reveals that the soul's destiny is not circular, but **ascent-based**—a sacred return to the heights from which it descended. The word *anagoge* refers to a mystical rising, a lifting up of the soul through inner purification, wisdom, and divine remembrance. In *Poimandres*, Hermes is shown the initial descent of the soul into matter, and then the stages of its return—through the planetary spheres, through self-liberation, and ultimately to divine reunion. This upward motion is not a reaction, but a **response to divine calling** from within the soul itself.

In *CH XIII*, Hermes guides his disciple in stripping away the lower vestments of the soul—the appetites, the illusions, the mortal memories. What remains is the essence of the divine self, which begins to **rise upward**, not by effort alone, but by the **lightness of truth**, which naturally lifts the soul back to the One. In *CH IV*, the Hermetic teachings emphasize that the wise are those who know their origin, and from this knowledge, they are drawn upward like fire to its source.

The Law of Anagoge reveals that ascent is not movement in space, but **alignment of being**. The soul rises by **becoming light**, by vibrating with the substance of its origin. This path is hidden to the senses, yet open to the awakened spirit. The more the soul remembers its divine identity, the more gravity releases its hold, and the upward path reveals itself—not as a destination, but as a **natural return to the Real**.

LAW 23: THE LAW OF THE GENERATIVE WORD (LOGISMOS)

Source: *Corpus Hermeticum VIII, CH XI, CH I (Poimandres)*

In Hermeticism, *Logismos* refers to the **generative Word or Reason**—the divine principle through which thought becomes form. This law reveals that **speech and thought are not passive**; they are acts of creation. The universe itself was generated by the Logos, and man—created in the image of the All—shares in this **power of creative utterance**.

Every word, every thought, is a **seed planted in the field of becoming**. Purified, it builds divine order. Impure, it breeds distortion. Thus, the Hermetic initiate learns to guard his thoughts and speech as sacred instruments of divine will.

Hermetic Insight

"The Word is a father to the act. As God spoke, the world became. As you think, so shall you shape."
(*Corpus Hermeticum VIII*)

"The Logos is the craftsman of the world. Through Him, all things were made and are still being made."
(*CH I, Poimandres*)

> "Man is the speaker of creation, for his logismos mirrors the divine."
> *(CH XI)*

Implication

This law teaches that **your word is a wand**, and your thought is a chisel. You are always shaping reality—whether consciously or unconsciously. The Hermetic path demands that you **speak only from the higher mind**, and that you wield your logismos as the gods do—with clarity, truth, and love.

This law is drawn from *Corpus Hermeticum VIII, CH XI, and CH I (Poimandres)*, where Hermes reveals that creation is not formed through matter first, but through **Word—Logismos**—the intelligent utterance of divine thought. In *Poimandres*, Hermes witnesses that before anything came into being, there was **Mind**, and from that Mind, there issued **Word**—a **living principle**, not simply spoken but *generated* with power. This generative Word becomes the **intermediary force**, shaping the invisible into the visible, giving form to essence, and order to chaos.

In *CH VIII*, Hermes explains that the soul must come to understand not just how to speak, but how to **speak in alignment with the divine pattern**. Words are not casual in the Hermetic tradition—they are **formative energies**, capable of creating reality. Each true Word carries within it a vibration that either brings one closer to the divine or binds one deeper into illusion.

CH XI builds further: the Word is the bridge between knowing and being. It is the expression of inner gnosis as outer force. To speak truth is not merely to describe reality—it is to **generate it**.

Thus, the Law of the Generative Word teaches that the initiate must guard the tongue, refine the mind, and speak only from **inner clarity**. Every Word has power to create, sustain, or destroy. The Logos is not simply the Divine Word—it is also the **inner logismos**, the reasoned soul, and it must be purified. When aligned, the initiate becomes one who speaks **with the voice of order**, who generates not from desire, but from harmony with the eternal blueprint.

LAW 24: THE LAW OF THE HIDDEN FIRE (PNEUMA)

Source: *Corpus Hermeticum IX, CH V, CH XIII*

The Hermetica speaks of **Pneuma**—the divine breath or **spiritual fire** that animates all life. This *hidden fire* is not physical flame, but the **vital, intelligent force** that pulses through the cosmos, the soul, and all living beings. It is the divine current that moves through the heart, awakens the mind, and gives birth to light within.

This fire is both **transcendent and immanent**—it is in the stars and in your breath. It is the living essence of the Divine, latent in all things, waiting to be **awakened by inner recognition and purity**.

Hermetic Insight

"The Pneuma is the breath of God, the secret fire that enlivens the cosmos and burns in the soul of man."
(*Corpus Hermeticum IX*)

"There is a fire in man that cannot be seen—it is the cause of movement, thought, and vision. It is the spirit of the Divine."
(*CH V*)

"The soul, when purified, becomes luminous. For the Pneuma burns within it, making it like unto the gods."
(*CH XIII*)

Implication

This law reveals that **divinity is not distant—it burns inside you**. When you cultivate inner silence, discipline, and vision, the Pneuma awakens. You feel it as clarity, power, and sacred heat. It is your eternal fire—hidden, but always present, waiting to ignite your return to the All.

This law is drawn from *Corpus Hermeticum IX, CH V, and CH XIII*, where Hermes reveals the mystery of **pneuma**, the **divine breath or spirit**, often referred to as the **hidden fire** within the human being. Unlike the visible fire of the elements, this fire is **invisible**, yet it animates all things. In *CH IX*, Hermes declares that nothing lives without **soul**, and nothing is animated without **pneuma**—a subtle flame hidden in all forms, even in stone and plant, but brightest in the human soul. This fire is the signature of divinity, **implanted in the heart of creation**.

In *CH V*, the sacred fire is portrayed as the **true self**, veiled beneath layers of flesh, thought, and emotion. It is the **divine light trapped within matter**, yearning for its return to the Source. In *CH XIII*, this pneuma is awakened through purification, contemplation, and spiritual rebirth. When the soul peels away its outer layers—its elemental garments—it begins to glow with the light of pneuma, and the hidden fire once dormant becomes a **torch of divine remembrance**.

This law teaches that the path to illumination does not require outside fire—it requires that the initiate recognize the **flame already burning within**. The fire of pneuma is the living essence of God in the soul: it does not consume, but **enlightens**. It does not destroy, but **reveals**. To live according to this law is to nourish that fire through inner stillness, devotion, and alignment—until the soul itself becomes **a lamp of divine consciousness**, capable of lighting the path for others.

LAW 25: THE LAW OF THE ETERNAL RETURN

Source: *Corpus Hermeticum I (Poimandres), CH X, CH XIII*

All emanations from the One eventually return to the One. This is the great Hermetic circle: **from unity, into multiplicity, and back into unity**. Every soul, every star, every form is caught in this divine rhythm. Nothing is lost—everything that descends into time must one day ascend back into eternity.

The Hermetica presents the cosmos not as linear, but **cyclical and spiraled**—forever unfolding, collapsing, and renewing. Rebirth, ascent, dissolution, and return are the sacred breathing of the universe.

Hermetic Insight

"From the One, all things have come; to the One, all things shall return. This is the nature of life and death, creation and dissolution."
(*Poimandres, CH I*)

"Everything that departs from unity shall seek it again. The soul that remembers shall rise; the soul that forgets shall return in time."
(*CH XIII*)

"There is no end to the circle, my child—only return. And in return, there is resurrection."
(*CH X*)

Implication

This law offers the ultimate comfort and challenge: **you cannot be lost, but you can be delayed**. The eternal return is both grace and law. All that is scattered must be gathered. All that is born must be reborn. Your journey is not a race, but a return—to Source, to Light, to the Divine Self.

This law is drawn from *Corpus Hermeticum I (Poimandres), CH X, and CH XIII*, where Hermes is shown that all things in the universe follow a sacred pattern: a **movement outward from the One**, and a **return inward to the One**. In *Poimandres*, Hermes witnesses the soul's descent into form, through the planetary spheres, and its eventual return—if purified—back to its divine origin. This is not reincarnation as mere repetition, but a **spiral of ascent**, where each cycle of embodiment offers the soul an opportunity to awaken further to its divine identity.

In *CH X*, Hermes reveals that this return is woven into the nature of the cosmos itself: every created thing carries within it the signature of its source and is drawn back to that source like fire to flame. In *CH XIII*, the return becomes conscious—as the initiate sheds the layers of illusion and rises through the celestial gates, the soul becomes aware that it has **never truly been separate**. The return is not a journey through space, but a **realization of oneness** that dissolves the illusion of exile.

The Law of the Eternal Return teaches that all souls, regardless of path, are being drawn back to the **center of divine unity**. Even those lost in shadow are being carried —knowingly or unknowingly—on the breath of return. The universe is not a machine—it is a **living cycle of divine memory**, calling all things back into alignment. The initiate, awakened to this truth, no longer fears death, time, or separation. They understand that **to return is to fulfill the very reason for which they were emanated**: to become conscious of the All and to rejoin it **not in ignorance, but in light**.

26. THE LAW OF DIVINE MEMORY

Source: *Corpus Hermeticum I (Poimandres), CH XIII, CH XI*

The Hermetica teaches that **the soul's fall into matter is a fall into forgetfulness**. It forgets its divine origin, its cosmic nature, and its sacred purpose. But the seed of truth is never lost—only buried. The work of the initiate is to awaken **divine memory**, the inward recollection of who and what one truly is.

This is not memory of past events, but of **eternal identity**. The moment you remember, you are reborn. This is why gnosis is often described as **anamnesis**—*remembrance of the divine*.

Hermetic Insight

"You have forgotten who you are, O soul. You were divine, born of light, clothed in immortality—and now you sleep in shadow. Awaken, and remember."
(*Poimandres, CH I*)

"The soul that remembers ascends; the soul that forgets is drawn again into birth. Remembrance is the first resurrection."
(*CH XIII*)

"Let your mind be silent, and you shall recall the truth not learned, but always known."
(*CH XI*)

Implication

This law teaches that your task is not to become something new, but to **remember what you have always been**. All wisdom, all power, all divinity is already within you, waiting for remembrance. This is the sacred wound of humanity—and the sacred healing: to **remember the divine within**.

This law is drawn from *Corpus Hermeticum I (Poimandres), CH XIII, and CH XI*, where Hermes reveals that the soul is not simply born in time, but carries within it the **imprint of eternity**. Before its descent into the material world, the soul beheld the Divine directly—immersed in the Light and aware of its Source. Upon embodiment, this memory is **veiled**, yet it is never lost. In *Poimandres*, Hermes is shown that the path of awakening begins when the soul **remembers** what it has always known: that it is a child of the Divine Mind, fashioned in the likeness of the All.

In *CH XI*, this divine memory is described not as something acquired, but as something **recovered**. The soul does not gain wisdom—it **recalls it**. Spiritual knowledge is not taught, but **unveiled from within**, as layers of forgetfulness are stripped away through purification and contemplation. This remembrance is not mental—it is **existential**. When divine memory is restored, the soul recognizes itself not as a product of the world, but as a **reflection of the eternal light**.

The Law of Divine Memory teaches that the highest truths cannot be given from without—they must be **reawakened from within**. The initiate's task is not to accumulate knowledge, but to **peel back the veils** that obscure the soul's original knowing. True gnosis is the moment the soul says: **"I remember who I am."** In that remembrance, separation ends. The light once known is known again, and the soul returns to its rightful place—**not as student, but as son and daughter of the Divine.**

LAW 27: THE LAW OF THE UNSEEN HAND (PROVIDENCE AND NECESSITY)

Source: *Corpus Hermeticum XII, CH X, CH XI*

The Hermetica reveals that the cosmos is governed not by blind fate, but by the intertwined forces of **Providence** (divine intention) and **Necessity** (cosmic order). Providence is the **unseen hand of the Divine Mind**, always guiding creation toward its perfection. Necessity is the **framework through which this guidance is expressed** —the law-bound structure of the visible and invisible realms.

Even apparent chaos is under the sway of these two forces. They are the **right and left hands of God**—Providence designs the good, and Necessity ensures it is fulfilled, often through challenge, discipline, or delay.

Hermetic Insight

"All things are moved by Providence and bound by Necessity. Nothing is outside of God's order—not even what seems unjust, for it too serves the good."
(*Corpus Hermeticum XII*)

"The world unfolds not by chance, but by divine thought. What appears crooked shall be straightened in time, for the hand of God is steady."
(*CH X*)

> **"He who knows Providence walks in peace. He who resists Necessity suffers needlessly."**
> (*CH XI*)

Implication

This law teaches deep trust: that **everything unfolds in accordance with divine mind**, even when obscured. By aligning with Providence through inner vision and accepting Necessity with grace, the initiate walks the path of wisdom. The more you resist, the more you suffer; the more you trust, the more you rise.

This law is drawn from *Corpus Hermeticum XII, CH X, and CH XI*, where Hermes unveils the interplay of two great forces that govern the cosmos: **Providence** and **Necessity**. In these dialogues, Hermes explains that the universe is not driven by chaos or blind fate, but by an **unseen hand**—a divine intelligence that orders all things. **Providence (Pronoia)** is the guiding force of the Divine Mind, the intentional, benevolent order that sustains and directs all life. **Necessity (Ananke)** is the chain of cause and effect through which that divine will is realized within the realm of time and matter.

In *CH XII*, Hermes teaches that while Providence reflects the **higher purpose of the All**, Necessity ensures that this purpose unfolds within the limitations of the created world. It is not bondage, but **law**—the structure through which cosmic harmony expresses itself. In *CH XI*, Hermes reminds us that the wise must discern between what is governed by divine intention and what arises from the constraints of material law. Those who awaken to this distinction do not rebel against Necessity—they **cooperate with it**, seeing it as the visible arm of the invisible will.

The Law of the Unseen Hand reveals that what seems accidental or fated is, in truth, **woven into a greater pattern**. To live in wisdom is to trust the invisible architecture of existence. The soul that perceives Providence beneath every necessity walks in peace, even amid storms. The initiate does not resist the hand of life, but aligns with its rhythm—knowing that behind every appearance lies the **breath of divine order**, always moving the soul toward its highest end.

LAW 28: THE LAW OF THE SACRED BODY (TEMPLE OF THE SOUL)

Source: *Corpus Hermeticum IV, CH X, Asclepius*

The Hermetica affirms that the **body is not a prison**, but a **temple**—a sacred dwelling place for the divine soul. While many traditions treat the body as something to be escaped or denied, Hermeticism honors it as a **living vessel**, shaped by the cosmos, infused with spirit, and capable of being transfigured into light.

The body holds divine architecture: it reflects the heavens, the elements, and the invisible forces of creation. It is to be purified, honored, and disciplined—not because it is base, but because it is **holy ground**.

Hermetic Insight

"Do not despise the body, my child—it is the dwelling of the soul, and the image of the cosmos. Within it are stars and gods and the laws of heaven."
(*Corpus Hermeticum IV*)

"Man is a temple, and within his heart the divine flame burns. If the body is cleansed, the soul may dwell there in peace and speak the Word."
(*CH X*)

> "In the body are mysteries hidden from the eyes. Its form was shaped by heaven, and through it the divine works in the world."
> (*Asclepius*)

Implication

This law reclaims the sacredness of incarnation. Your body is not an obstacle to enlightenment—it is **part of the path**. To purify the body, to align it with divine law, is to make it a **living temple** where spirit may dwell fully. Treat it as such, and it becomes not your cage, but your chariot.

This law is drawn from *Corpus Hermeticum IV, CH X*, and the *Asclepius*, where Hermes teaches that the human body is not merely a vessel of flesh but a **sacred temple**, constructed by divine intelligence as the dwelling place of the soul. In *CH IV*, Hermes describes the human being as the image of the cosmos itself—a **microcosm**, containing within the structure of the body the same order, harmony, and elemental composition as the universe. The body, far from being a prison, is a **sanctuary**, built to house the soul and to reflect the divine mind in motion.

In the *Asclepius*, this teaching is brought into fuller form: the body is described as a **living altar**, where the rituals of life, thought, breath, and action become offerings to the Divine. It is in the body that the soul learns, remembers, and transforms. Each limb, organ, and breath is a correspondence to the greater celestial body above.

Thus, to care for the body, purify it, and use it in service of higher realization is not vanity—it is a **sacred responsibility**.

This law reminds the initiate that **matter is not fallen**—it is divine in origin and purpose. The body is not to be denied, but **consecrated**. Through discipline, harmony, and reverence, the body becomes a **living temple**, where the flame of spirit may burn clearly. The sacred work of the soul cannot be done apart from the body—it must be done *through* it. The law teaches that the path of transformation is not only inward, but **embodied**. The soul must learn to dwell in its temple with honor, so that it may one day ascend from it in glory.

LAW 29: THE LAW OF THE GENERATIVE LIGHT

Source: *Corpus Hermeticum I (Poimandres), CH XIII, CH V*

All things are brought into being through **Light**—not physical light, but the **generative light of the Divine Mind**. This is the first substance, the radiant essence of creation. It shines through Nous, reflects through the Logos, and animates the cosmos. Everything that lives, moves, or exists **is made of light in some form**.

In man, this light is the **inner flame**, the spark of the divine that seeks to return to its source. As the soul purifies itself, this inner light grows stronger, until the soul itself becomes **a being of light**, radiant and eternal.

Hermetic Insight

"I saw a great light—boundless, joyful, and alive. And from that light came a holy Word, and from the Word, creation."
(*Poimandres, CH I*)

"There is a light in the soul, brighter than the sun, though hidden by desire and illusion. When you find it, you will see the Divine."
(*CH V*)

"You have become light, my child, and with light you shall return. For only light may enter the dwelling of the gods."
(CH XIII)

Implication

This law affirms that **you are not made of dust alone—you are made of light**. Your task is to remove what dims it. Everything sacred—truth, vision, love—flows from this generative light. To walk the Hermetic path is to **live as a bearer of light**, becoming luminous in thought, word, and soul.

This law is drawn from *Corpus Hermeticum I (Poimandres), CH XIII,* and *CH V*, where Hermes is shown the mystery of **divine light as the generative force** behind all creation. In *Poimandres*, the birth of the cosmos begins not with form, but with **light—a living, intelligent radiance** that emerges from the womb of divine darkness. This light is not inert illumination; it is **active, fecund, and shaping**. It gives form to thought and movement to stillness. It is the first expression of divine will—the **seed of all becoming**.

In *CH XIII*, the generative nature of light is made personal. Hermes guides the initiate through an inner transformation, where the soul sheds its lower garments and becomes **luminous**, filled with the **light that begets divinity within**. This inner illumination is not metaphorical—it is **ontological**. The soul begins to shine with the very light from which it was born. In *CH V*, light is revealed as the **subtle thread** that binds the worlds together, the medium through which spirit penetrates matter, and the pathway by which the soul may rise.

The Law of the Generative Light teaches that light is not the byproduct of enlightenment—it is the **cause** of it. The initiate must not merely seek the light, but become **a source of it**, letting their thoughts, words, and deeds shine with creative power. This light, once ignited, does not merely illuminate—it **generates**: it creates harmony, births wisdom, and awakens others. To align with this law is to participate in the original act of creation—to become, in the inner world, what the Divine Light was in the beginning: **the bringer of order, life, and truth.**

LAW 30: THE LAW OF DIVINE SILENCE (THE INEFFABLE)

Source: *Corpus Hermeticum II, CH V, CH XI*

There is a point where all words must fall silent. The deepest mysteries of the Divine—the essence of the One, the Source beyond being—are **ineffable**, beyond thought, language, or image. This is the **Law of Divine Silence**, which teaches that ultimate truth is not spoken, but experienced in **stillness**.

The Hermetica often ends or begins its highest revelations with a call to **reverent silence**, where the initiate withdraws from all outer noise and enters into sacred communion with the Unknowable.

In this silence, the soul becomes a mirror for the divine. Not by speaking, but by **being**.

Hermetic Insight

"**The One is beyond name, beyond form, beyond thought. To speak of It is to veil It. To know It, be silent.**"
(*Corpus Hermeticum II*)

"**Cease from all argument, O soul, and be still. For in silence, the Father is known.**"
(*CH V*)

"I shall not speak further, for I have touched the Ineffable. Let silence now speak where words fail."
(*CH XI*)

Implication

This law is your final threshold: when the soul has climbed every sphere, uttered every prayer, and released every form, **only silence remains**. And in that silence, the All is heard. To practice this law is to enter the holy of holies—to become still enough to contain the voice of God within.

This law is drawn from *Corpus Hermeticum II, CH V,* and *CH XI*, where Hermes speaks of that which lies **beyond all speech, image, and concept**—the **Ineffable**, known only in **Divine Silence**. In *CH II*, Hermes is told that while the Divine Mind (Nous) emanates the cosmos through thought and word, its **origin and essence remain veiled**, transcending all understanding. The All is knowable only through its emanations, but its **source**—its silent root—cannot be grasped by intellect or imagination.

In *CH V*, Hermes teaches that the soul must move past reason, past language, and even past knowing, to enter into **pure contact** with the Divine. This contact is not an event of thought—it is a **state of presence**, a merging in which all distinctions dissolve. In *CH XI*, he refers to this as the **silent truth**, which can only be received in stillness, when the soul is stripped of all motion, all desire to name, control, or define.

The Law of Divine Silence teaches that the **highest knowledge is not knowledge at all**, but direct communion with the One. Just as noise ceases for music to be heard inwardly, so too must speech cease for **truth to reveal itself in its fullness**. The initiate who has passed through all layers of word, form, and vibration arrives at this silent threshold—not in ignorance, but in reverent surrender. In this sacred stillness, the soul comes to dwell not in the light of understanding, but in the **darkness of knowing beyond knowing**. This is the mystery of the Ineffable: not to be spoken, only to be **entered**.

LAW 31: THE LAW OF DIVINE CONTAINMENT (THE ALL IN ALL)

Source: *Corpus Hermeticum II, CH XI, CH IX*

In the most sacred passages of the Hermetica, we are told that **God is not merely in all things—God is all things**. There is **nothing outside the All**, and yet the All is fully contained in every part. This is not poetic language—it is metaphysical truth: **the Whole is present in the part**, and the Divine contains, sustains, and permeates every level of existence simultaneously.

This law affirms the principle of **holographic divinity**: that each soul, each point in space, each atom is a doorway into the All—not symbolically, but actually.

Hermetic Insight

"**God is an infinite sphere, whose center is everywhere and circumference nowhere. He is within all things, and yet all things are in Him.**"
(*Corpus Hermeticum II*)

"**He is not distant, nor does He exist in some separate place. The Father is everywhere, in everything, always, and yet above all.**"
(*CH XI*)

"You ask where God is? In you, in me, in all—yet in none as separate. The All is One, and One is All."
(CH IX)

Implication

This law destroys the illusion of distance between the seeker and the divine. You are **already within the All**, and the All is within you. To awaken is to **recognize this eternal containment**—that every moment, every breath, and every thought occurs within the very substance of God.

This law is drawn from *Corpus Hermeticum II, CH XI*, and *CH IX*, where Hermes receives one of the most profound teachings of the Hermetic tradition: that **the Divine is in all things, and all things are within the Divine**. In *CH II*, Hermes is shown that the All is not something outside creation, nor is creation outside of it. Instead, there is a mystery of **mutual containment**—a paradox in which the Divine both permeates and embraces the totality of existence. Every point in the cosmos contains the fullness of the One, and yet the One also transcends the totality.

In *CH XI*, Hermes is led to contemplate how the Divine does not reside in a place or direction—it is everywhere and nowhere, wholly present in the smallest atom and fully expressed in the vastness of the stars. In *CH IX*, the teaching becomes even more intimate: the soul, too, contains the All, and thus to know oneself is to know the Divine. The initiate who sees clearly recognizes that **there** is no separation between Creator and creation. Everything is held within a **living, divine field of presence**.

The Law of Divine Containment teaches that all attempts to seek the Divine elsewhere must eventually fall away. The All is not hidden—it is **immanent**, quietly saturating every moment, every breath, every form. The wise do not ascend by fleeing the world, but by recognizing that **each part of it is a reflection of the whole**. To live according to this law is to carry reverence into every encounter, to speak with the knowledge that **every other is the One in disguise**, and to realize that **the Divine is nearer than thought—closer than being—within and around all, eternally.

LAW 32: THE LAW OF ETERNAL SIMULTANEITY (TIME AS THOUGHT)

Source: *Corpus Hermeticum XI, CH X, CH I (Poimandres)*

Time, in the Hermetic sense, is not a river—it is a **construct of mind**. The Divine does not move through time; it **contains all time** within a single eternal moment. Past, present, and future are modes of **perception**, not divisions in reality.

In its deepest metaphysics, the Hermetica teaches that **the All exists simultaneously**, that **creation did not happen—it is happening**, eternally sustained by divine thought. What appears sequential in the world is **instantaneous in the mind of the One**.

Hermetic Insight

"In God, all is now. There is no future, no past. All things are fully present, fully complete, fully alive in one thought."
(*Corpus Hermeticum XI*)

"Time is the moving image of eternity, distorted by the senses. The soul that rises perceives that all things have already been."
(*CH X*)

> "The cosmos was created in a single thought, and that thought is still occurring."
> (*Poimandres, CH I*)

Implication

This law unveils that **you are not bound by linearity**. When you ascend in consciousness, you leave behind the illusion of sequence and step into **the eternal Now**—a domain where vision, memory, and destiny collapse into one. It is in this **eternal simultaneity** that divine insight arises.

This law is drawn from *Corpus Hermeticum XI, CH X*, and *CH I (Poimandres)*, where Hermes receives the revelation that **time is not a river, but a function of perception**—a movement within thought itself. In *Poimandres*, Hermes sees the soul descend into time through the celestial spheres, acquiring sensation, motion, and the illusion of sequence. Yet as it returns, it reenters a state where all things are perceived **not in order, but in wholeness**. This is eternity—not infinite duration, but the **absence of before and after**. The Divine dwells not in time, but in the **eternal now**, and so too does the awakened soul.

In *CH XI*, Hermes learns that all temporal things are reflections of **eternal archetypes** held within Divine Mind. What appears as past, present, and future is, in truth, a projection of consciousness. **Time is the shadow of thought moving,** and when thought is still, time dissolves. In *CH X*, it is revealed that the wise can live within time without being bound by it—**seeing all events as already fulfilled within the Divine pattern**, and therefore walking with peace, precision, and power.

The Law of Eternal Simultaneity teaches that time is a lens, not a law. It does not flow independently of the observer—it arises from the **soul's descent into motion and multiplicity**. The initiate who begins to ascend through contemplation and inner stillness touches the edge of eternity, where all events, all beings, and all truths are **present at once**, and the burden of sequence is lifted. To live in alignment with this law is to release anxiety, to trust in divine timing, and to perceive that every moment contains the **entirety of creation**—not unfolding, but **already whole**.

LAW 33: THE LAW OF RECURSIVE CREATION (THE CREATOR CREATES THE CREATOR)

Source: *Corpus Hermeticum I (Poimandres), CH II, CH XI*

The Hermetica contains one of the deepest metaphysical revelations: **the Creator is not fixed—it recreates itself through its own emanations**. Divine Mind (Nous) gives birth to Logos (Word), which in turn **generates worlds and souls**, and through the ascent of awakened souls, **the Divine is renewed in itself**.

This is **recursive creation**: the One produces the Many, and the Many return to the One, not just as themselves—but **as new expressions of the divine**. Thus, God not only creates, but **becomes more God through creation**.

Hermetic Insight

"The Nous, which is God, brought forth the Logos, and the Logos shaped the cosmos. And from the cosmos arose the souls, and from the awakened souls, God came to know Himself again."
(*Poimandres, CH I*)

"God is a mind in motion, eternally giving birth to itself through all beings. The end is the beginning, and the beginning is the end."
(*CH II*)

"He who knows himself, knows the All. And he who knows the All, returns it to the One."
(CH XI)

Implication

This law unveils the sacred task of the soul: **not only to return to God, but to return God to Himself**. The Divine created you so that, through you, it could become more conscious of its own perfection. You are not a passive creation—you are a **mirror in which the Creator sees itself anew**.

This law is drawn from *Corpus Hermeticum I (Poimandres), CH II,* and *CH XI,* where Hermes is initiated into one of the most sacred mysteries of the Hermetic tradition: **creation is not linear**—it is **recursive**, a sacred loop in which the **Creator brings forth beings capable of creating**, and in turn, those beings give rise to **new expressions of the Divine**. In *Poimandres*, Hermes witnesses the emanation of the cosmos from the Light and Mind of God. From this Mind issues another being, the **Anthropos**, made in the image of the Divine—a self-conscious force that mirrors the Creator and is **endowed with creative power**.

In *CH II*, Hermes is taught that this Anthropos, though emanated, is not lesser—it is a **co-creative principle**, capable of descending into matter, organizing forms, and giving birth to new realities. It is in this that the cosmos becomes **alive**, because it is not only formed by God—it **continues to be formed by the divine beings God brings**

forth. And in *CH XI*, this recursive unfolding is revealed to be eternal: what is born of the Divine returns to the Divine, carrying with it new light, new thought, and new creative potency.

The Law of Recursive Creation teaches that you are not a creation in the passive sense—you are a **creator in the recursive sense**. You are not simply made by God—you are made **to become God-like**, to participate in the **ongoing genesis of being**. This law dissolves all notions of separation or subordination. The Divine births beings not to worship it from afar, but to **refract its power**, extend its reach, and magnify its presence through a chain of conscious co-creators. To awaken to this law is to realize that your destiny is not to reflect creation, but to **generate it anew**.

LAW 34: THE LAW OF REVERSED PERCEPTION (THE DESCENT IS ASCENT)

Source: *Corpus Hermeticum XII, CH VII, CH XIV*

What appears as **descent into matter** is, from a higher vision, **an ascent into divine realization**. The Hermetica teaches that the soul's embodiment is not a fall, but a **sacrifice made for the purpose of divine rediscovery**. Only through contact with limitation can the boundless be known. Thus, **matter is the mirror through which spirit comes to self-awareness**.

This is the paradox of initiation: to rise, you must first descend. To know spirit, you must confront form. Every veil you pass through was placed not to hide truth—but to awaken it.

Hermetic Insight

"The soul enters body not to be chained, but to be tested; not to be condemned, but to rise through its own remembrance."
(*CH XII*)

"Those who descend into the world with vision shall rise above it with power. For the world is the furnace of divinity."
(*CH VII*)

"The wise descend willingly, for they know that the road downward winds upward again."
(*CH XIV*)

Implication

This law transforms the meaning of suffering, limitation, and incarnation. You are not lost—you are **immersed in the proving ground of the gods**. What seems like a descent is the start of your **return ascent**. Every veil you lift expands the capacity of the divine to recognize itself through you.

This law is drawn from *Corpus Hermeticum XII, CH VII,* and *CH XIV*, where Hermes imparts a paradoxical truth at the heart of Hermetic initiation: what appears as **descent**—the soul's movement into body, matter, and limitation—is not a fall, but a **prelude to ascent**. In *CH XII*, Hermes teaches that the soul's incarnation is not a punishment, but a **necessary forgetting**, a sacred veil through which the soul may come to know the Divine **not by proximity, but by contrast**. To descend into matter is to enter the crucible in which **self-knowledge is forged**.

In *CH VII*, Hermes describes the human being as a divine creature who, though bound by flesh and time, is capable of **awakening to its source from within the shadows**. The soul, through its journey in the world, gathers not only experience but **weight**—and it is this weight that becomes the resistance through which spiritual muscle is built. In *CH XIV*, the teaching deepens: the path of return is not a rejection of embodiment, but a **realization of its divine function**. As the soul works through illusion, it becomes purified—not in spite of its descent, but because of it.

The Law of Reversed Perception teaches that the lowest is not the furthest from God—it is the mirror in which the Divine learns to behold itself. Descent is the **seed of return**, the arc of the journey that bends upward even as it moves downward. What seems like exile is the beginning of remembrance. The initiate who understands this no longer sees the world as a distraction, but as a **stairway built in reverse**. To ascend, one must descend **consciously**—carrying the divine flame into matter, and then lifting both back to their origin.

LAW 35: THE LAW OF HARMONIC RESONANCE (TUNING THE SOUL TO THE REAL)

Source: *Corpus Hermeticum XIV, CH VI, Asclepius (late passages)*

Reality is not known by observation—it is **recognized by resonance**. The Hermetica reveals that truth cannot be grasped unless the soul is **tuned to the same frequency as the Real**. The Divine is always speaking, but only the soul that has achieved internal harmony can **resonate with its signal**.

This tuning occurs through the alignment of thought, desire, and spirit with the **immutable harmony** of the cosmos. When the soul vibrates with this inner music, it knows—not by deduction, but by **direct attunement**.

Hermetic Insight

"**The soul must be made to resemble the things it seeks to know. For like is known only by like, and harmony speaks only to harmony.**"
(CH XIV)

"Those who have discord within cannot hear the voice of the divine. The universe sings, but only the tuned soul perceives its order."
(CH VI)

"What the senses cannot detect, the purified soul hears as music, and what was hidden becomes present."
(*Asclepius*)

Implication

This law teaches that gnosis is not mental—it is **musical**. To know the truth is to **resonate with it**, as a string vibrates in sympathy with another. The goal of initiation is to bring the soul into such perfect internal order that **it hums with the cosmos** and knows the Real by communion, not comparison.

This law is drawn from *Corpus Hermeticum XIV, CH VI,* and the late passages of the *Asclepius,* where Hermes reveals that the soul is not a fixed entity, but a **vibratory instrument**, capable of being tuned either to the illusions of the lower world or to the **harmony of the divine Real**. In *CH XIV*, Hermes explains that just as music requires the tuning of strings to express true tone, so too must the soul be tuned to the divine order to express its **original harmony**. The human being, as microcosm, is embedded within a universe of tones—each thought, desire, and perception creates a frequency that either aligns or clashes with the higher spheres.

In *CH VI*, Hermes teaches that error is the result of **dissonance**—a soul out of tune with its source. This discord manifests as confusion, suffering, and misalignment. But when the soul is disciplined through contemplation, truth, and reverence, it gradually retunes itself to the **eternal vibration of the One**. In the *Asclepius*, the world itself is said to be maintained by this hidden harmony—a cosmic music that sustains all being. The wise, Hermes teaches, are those who hear this music, not with the ears, but with the inner sense sharpened by virtue and vision.

The Law of Harmonic Resonance teaches that the path to gnosis is not intellectual alone—it is **vibrational**. The initiate does not learn the Real—they **become attuned** to it. Every act of purification is a tuning. Every alignment of thought, emotion, and action is a movement toward inner resonance with the Divine. When the soul is fully harmonized, it no longer seeks truth outside—it becomes a **living echo of truth**, vibrating in unity with the music of the spheres. In that sacred resonance, the soul finds peace —not as escape, but as **attunement to the eternal chord that holds all worlds together**.

LAW 36: THE LAW OF SACRED DENSITY (THE WISDOM OF EMBODIED LIGHT)

Source: *Corpus Hermeticum VII, CH XIV, Asclepius (middle passages)*

In Hermetic cosmology, **density is not deficiency**—it is *compressed intelligence*. The descent of light into form is not a corruption of purity, but a **sacramental act of embodiment**. The more concentrated the light, the more **wisdom it holds in hidden form**.

The body, the world, and matter itself are **densified expressions of divine will**—the outer bark of inner fire. The initiate is taught not to reject the dense, but to read its **inner script**—to extract luminous insight from the densest expressions of being.

Hermetic Insight

"**Do not curse the weight of the world, for within it is stored the seed of heaven. Heavy is the fruit that nourishes.**"
(CH VII)

"All things contain the divine, even in darkness. Matter is the slow speech of the divine mind—listen carefully, and you shall understand."
(CH XIV)

"In body is mystery, in stone is memory, in earth is law. The density is the veil—but the veil is holy."
(*Asclepius*)

Implication

This law reveals that every layer of density—matter, emotion, time—is a **slowed frequency of light**, containing wisdom only the still and reverent can hear. Your task is not to escape embodiment, but to **draw its divine content upward**, to interpret the dense as scripture carved in the language of light.

This law is drawn from *Corpus Hermeticum VII, CH XIV,* and the middle passages of the *Asclepius,* where Hermes reveals that matter is not a fall from spirit but a **condensation of divine light**—a sacred density through which wisdom is made visible. In *CH VII*, Hermes describes the cosmos as formed by Nous (Divine Mind), which "wrapped itself in a robe of fire and water," becoming both luminous and substantial. This teaches that embodiment is not a descent into illusion, but a **revelation through form**—a divine thought made tangible.

In *CH XIV*, Hermes affirms that the Divine is not distant from the world but **intimately woven into its texture**. The heavier the veil, the more potential there is for light to be discovered within. The *Asclepius* develops this further: the physical world is described as a "sacred image" (statua sacra), where spirit and body are **not in conflict**, but in creative tension. The body becomes a **container for divine**

intelligence, and density is the very condition that allows the invisible to become knowable.

The Law of Sacred Density teaches that light does not diminish when it enters form—it **deepens**. Matter is the mirror through which light perceives itself from within. Embodiment is not a limitation, but an opportunity for the soul to **learn, refine, and express** its inner divinity through structure and resistance. The initiate who understands this law does not reject the body or the material world but approaches both with reverence, knowing that **the densest realities may conceal the deepest truths**. Embodied light is not less than divine light—it is **divine light fulfilled**.

LAW 37: THE LAW OF THE INFINITE INTERIOR (DEPTH OVER DISTANCE)

Source: *Corpus Hermeticum VI, CH IX, Asclepius (deep structure passages)*

In the Hermetic system, space is not sacred because of its vastness, but because of its **depth**. True divinity is not found by **reaching outward**, but by **descending inward**. The deeper the soul travels within itself, the closer it comes to **the origin of all things**—for the center of the soul is the center of the cosmos.

Hermes reveals that **infinity is not a matter of scale, but of interiority**. The mysteries of the stars and the gods are **imprinted within**, and can only be accessed by penetrating the innermost chamber of being.

Hermetic Insight

"If you would find the origin of all, do not look to the stars but to your own center, for the deep is within, not above."
(*CH VI*)

"The inward path is the path to God. The outer heavens are symbols; the true sky is the soul's interior."
(*CH IX*)

> "In the smallest part of yourself lies the whole. The divine hides in depth, not distance."
> (*Asclepius*)

Implication

This law inverts the seeker's gaze: **you are not far from the divine—you are layered from it**. Each veil is a depth, and each depth a gate. To find the All, you must go inward beyond identity, thought, even light itself—until you reach the **primordial stillness that precedes creation**, hidden within you since before time.

This law is drawn from *Corpus Hermeticum VI, CH IX*, and the deeper structural teachings within the *Asclepius*, where Hermes shifts the aspirant's gaze from outward ascent to **inward depth**. In *CH VI*, Hermes teaches that truth is not found by moving through space, climbing levels, or reaching distant heights—it is accessed by going **inward**, into the unfathomable **depth of the soul**, where the Divine dwells in silence. The cosmos, he says, is vast, but the soul contains mysteries **greater than the stars**, for it is made in the likeness of the One.

In *CH IX*, Hermes reinforces that the soul must cultivate **interiority**, not as isolation but as the only place where true gnosis can emerge. The initiate who endlessly seeks externally remains in motion, while the one who turns inward reaches the **still center**, where all is present. In the *Asclepius*, the soul is described as a temple with many inner chambers. The Divine does not reside in the outer court of the world, but in the **innermost sanctum** of being, hidden in depth, not in distance.

The Law of the Infinite Interior teaches that the path to the Divine is **not linear**, but vertical inward. Eternity is not beyond the stars—it is behind the veil of one's own heart. To seek far is to miss what lies near. As the initiate descends inward, the soul passes through layers of memory, fear, false identity—until, in the core, it touches **infinity folded within**. This is the paradox of the Hermetic path: the highest ascent is made by those who go **deep enough to find the root of all things**, which has always lived within them.

Law 38: The Law of Sacred Irreversibility (The Seal of Becoming)

Source: *Corpus Hermeticum XIII, CH XIV, Asclepius (concluding revelations)*

There is a moment in the path of the initiate where a transformation occurs that **cannot be undone**. It is not knowledge—it is *being*. The Hermetica teaches that once the soul **truly becomes divine**, it is **sealed** with a spiritual mark that prevents return to ignorance. This is **sacred irreversibility**: a threshold crossed not by effort, but by identity.

The soul that has truly *become* cannot unbecome. Just as fire cannot become wood again, the illumined cannot return to darkness—not because they are forbidden, but because they **no longer exist as what they once were**.

Hermetic Insight

"When the soul becomes divine, it receives the seal of the heavens. It cannot descend again, for it has changed its nature."
(CH XIII)

"This mystery, once entered, cannot be departed. You do not return as who you were—you are born again, and the old name is lost."
(CH XIV)

"He who has touched the incorruptible is forever altered. Time and death pass him by."
(*Asclepius*)

Implication

This law declares that spiritual transformation is **not reversible opinion—it is ontological rebirth**. The one who reaches gnosis cannot unknow, because **he no longer is the one who did not know**. Your destiny is not an achievement, but a metamorphosis—sealed by the divine itself, beyond return.

This law is drawn from *Corpus Hermeticum XIII, CH XIV,* and the *concluding revelations of the Asclepius*, where Hermes unveils the mystery of **permanent transformation**—the irreversible shift that occurs when the soul passes through true spiritual rebirth. In *CH XIII*, Hermes guides Tat through the stages of inner purification until the soul becomes "God instead of mortal." This metamorphosis is not symbolic—it is **ontological**, marking a point beyond which the soul **cannot return to ignorance**, for it has sealed itself with the **essence of becoming**.

In *CH XIV*, this transformation is revealed to carry a **sacred finality**. Just as gold cannot return to lead, the soul, once transmuted by divine fire, is no longer subject to the cycles of illusion and bondage. It has become fixed—not in stagnation, but in **eternal clarity**. The *Asclepius* echoes this in its final teachings, where Hermes speaks of a future humanity destined to fall into forgetfulness. Yet those who have **truly awakened**, he says, will remain as "gods among men," untouched by decay, bearing the **seal of the Real** within their nature.

The Law of Sacred Irreversibility teaches that there is a moment—often unseen, but utterly real—when the soul crosses a threshold from **seeking to being**, from **movement to arrival**. This is not a plateau, but a **permanent anchoring in truth**, after which the soul no longer wavers. It does not mean perfection of form, but **completion of identity**. The initiate who reaches this stage has become the thing they once pursued. And having become it, they no longer walk the path—they **are the path**.

LAW 39: THE LAW OF THE WORDLESS TRANSFER (TRANSMISSION THROUGH BEING)

Source: *Corpus Hermeticum VII, CH XIII, Asclepius (silent instruction dialogues)*

The Hermetica discloses that the highest truths cannot be taught through **explanation**, only through **transmission**—a wordless recognition that flows from **one awakened soul to another**. This is not instruction—it is **vibrational awakening**. The master transmits not facts, but *presence*, and the disciple receives not data, but *being*.

Such transfer occurs when two souls are aligned in silence. It is **knowing beyond voice**. The Logos is present, but **unspoken**—it travels through gaze, breath, nearness, and the still field of mutual recognition.

Hermetic Insight

"You ask for words, but what you need is presence. Let me sit beside you, and you shall receive more than speech."
(*CH VII*)

"The divine is not explained. It is transmitted, and the soul who is ready receives it in stillness."
(*CH XIII*)

"There are teachings that pass from heart to heart, untouched by tongue or ink. They are drawn in the air between us."
(*Asclepius*)

Implication

This law honors a mystery: **the soul does not awaken by argument, but by resonance with awakened being**. If you wish to teach the highest truths, you must become them. Speak less, radiate more. The greatest Hermetic instruction is given not by voice, but by the **wordless light you emit**.

This law is drawn from *Corpus Hermeticum VII, CH XIII*, and the silent instruction dialogues found in the *Asclepius*, where Hermes reveals that the highest knowledge is **not passed through words**, but through **presence**. In *CH VII*, Hermes explains that true wisdom cannot be taught in the ordinary sense—it must be **received in silence**, absorbed by the soul through **vibrational attunement** rather than conceptual instruction. The teacher may speak, but what is transmitted is not the sound of the teaching—it is the **essence of the teacher's being**, which awakens remembrance in the student.

In *CH XIII*, this is dramatically embodied in Hermes' initiation of Tat. While much is spoken, the transformation itself does not occur through words—it occurs in the **stillness between them**, when Tat experiences the radiance of his father's realization. In these moments, Tat receives something beyond doctrine—a **living flame** passed from soul to soul, without effort, without articulation. In the *Asclepius*, this is echoed in the moments of sacred silence that fall between questions and answers—where the deeper knowing is shared through **still presence** and **divine vibration**.

The Law of the Wordless Transfer teaches that being is the highest form of teaching. The initiate becomes a transmitter not by eloquence, but by **embodiment**. When one is truly aligned with the Real, their mere presence **radiates instruction**. The student receives not information, but **resonance**, a deep interior shift ignited by **proximity to awakened being**. This is the mystery behind all sacred lineages—not what was said, but what was silently **transferred**. To walk in this law is to understand that wisdom is not taught—it is **caught**.

LAW 40: THE LAW OF VEILED CLARITY (TRUTH HIDDEN BY REVELATION)

Source: *Corpus Hermeticum VI, CH XV, Asclepius (closing verses)*

In the Hermetic path, **truth does not hide behind obscurity—it hides in plain sight**. The divine veils itself not through riddles, but through **clarity too vast to comprehend at once**. Revelation itself becomes the veil, not by deception, but by excess.

This law teaches that **what blinds the unready is not darkness, but too much light**. The teachings are clear, but their clarity exceeds the vision of an unpurified soul. The Hermetica thus presents truth **through paradox, allegory, and poetic structure**—not to confuse, but to protect.

Hermetic Insight

"The divine does not conceal—it reveals beyond your seeing. The veil is in your eye, not in the Word."
(*CH VI*)

"Truth is open like the sky, but the blind curse it for being too wide. Narrow minds cannot hold the full."
(*CH XV*)

> "The gods teach by hiding in speech that seems simple. But beneath each line, a cosmos turns."
> (*Asclepius*)

Implication

This law reminds the initiate that **spiritual blindness is not from lack of revelation, but lack of readiness**. Your task is not to demand clearer signs, but to **enlarge your sight**. The highest truths are often **spoken simply, softly, and early—but only understood after the soul is made vast enough to see them**.

This law is drawn from *Corpus Hermeticum VI, CH XV,* and the *closing verses of the Asclepius*, where Hermes reveals a paradox central to Hermetic wisdom: **the more clearly truth is revealed, the more deeply it hides itself**. In *CH VI*, Hermes explains that divine teachings are not meant to be concealed through secrecy, but through **the overwhelming clarity of their nature**. Truth is veiled not by absence, but by presence—it shines so purely that the unprepared eye cannot discern it. Thus, even revelation becomes a kind of **concealment**, until the soul is purified enough to see.

In *CH XV*, this mystery is reinforced. Hermes warns that divine speech always contains **layers**, and that what appears as the surface meaning is only the outer garment of a deeper truth. The initiate must learn to see **through**, not just **at**. The *Asclepius* echoes this in its final verses, where the sacred teachings are entrusted to the worthy—

not because others are excluded, but because **clarity itself will blind the uninitiated**, and what is sacred must be **hidden in plain sight** until the eye of wisdom opens.

The Law of Veiled Clarity teaches that **revelation is not the end of the search, but its refinement**. Each unveiling reveals another veil, until the soul no longer seeks facts, but **enters into presence**. The initiate must not cling to words or symbols, but penetrate them—letting go of literalism to grasp the **living truth beneath form**. To live this law is to walk the path with humility, knowing that even the brightest light may cast the deepest shadow—and that the truest things are often hidden, not by obscurity, but by their unbearable simplicity.

LAW 41: THE LAW OF DOUBLE VISION (SEEING THE REAL BEHIND THE REAL)

Source: *Corpus Hermeticum XV, CH VI, Asclepius (doctrines on divine images)*

The Hermetica speaks to the development of a higher faculty—**double vision**—where the initiate perceives the **visible and the invisible simultaneously**. To the awakened soul, the world is not replaced, but **overlaid**—the physical is seen, and behind it, the **divine structure that sustains it**.

This second sight is not imagination; it is **the unveiling of depth** within form. Statues, bodies, stars, and voices become transparent, revealing the hidden intelligence moving through them. **Symbol and substance converge**.

Hermetic Insight

"He who sees only what is before him sees nothing. But he who sees through what is seen finds what cannot be spoken."
(CH XV)

"The gods have made the world a book. Read its face, but also read its fire beneath the letters."
(CH VI)

> "Statues are not dead forms—they are veils of force. The wise see the force, not just the shape."
> (*Asclepius*)

Implication

This law trains the soul to live in two worlds at once—not by splitting vision, but by **deepening it**. Reality is layered, and the Hermetic adept must learn to perceive both the **surface symbol** and the **inner essence** simultaneously. This is the beginning of true theurgy—**to see with the eyes of spirit while walking in the body of form**.

The Law of Double Vision (Seeing the Real Behind the Real)

This law is drawn from *Corpus Hermeticum XV, CH VI*, and the *Asclepius*—particularly the doctrines on divine images—where Hermes unveils the principle of **Double Vision**: the ability to see both **the surface of reality and the invisible essence behind it** simultaneously. In *CH VI*, Hermes explains that the outer forms of creation are **not illusions**, but **living symbols**, each bearing a deeper truth that only the awakened eye can perceive. To the uninitiated, the world appears literal and fixed. To the initiate, it is a veil **through which the divine constantly communicates**.

In *CH XV*, Hermes emphasizes that every appearance conceals a higher pattern—a divine archetype expressing itself through the material world. This does not mean the world is false, but that its **true nature is layered**. The *Asclepius* expands this mystery in its doctrine on statues and divine images, where physical forms are said to **contain spirit**, and sacred images are **not merely representations**, but **vessels through which divinity manifests**. To see with double vision is to **perceive the divine through the visible**—to recognize that every object, event, and person is a **portal** to the Real.

The Law of Double Vision teaches that the initiate must train the soul to look **beyond the surface** without denying it. It is not the rejection of appearances, but their **transfiguration**. What seems mundane becomes sacred. What appears ordinary becomes radiant. The world is not an obstacle to truth, but its **encrypted mirror**. To live by this law is to walk through the world with inner sight awakened—seeing form and essence, mask and face, image and source—as **one vision, doubled by wisdom**.

LAW 42: THE LAW OF SILENT REVERSAL (THE DESCENT OF THE DIVINE INTO YOU)

Source: *Corpus Hermeticum XV, CH XIII, Asclepius (doctrines of divine embodiment)*

As the soul ascends toward the Divine, there comes a sacred inversion—the **Divine descends into the soul**. This is not metaphor. The Hermetica teaches that at the highest stage of purification, when the seeker lets go of all seeking, **God enters**, silently and unannounced. This is the **reversal of the mystic current**: no longer do you ascend—**the All descends and abides within**.

This law is called "silent" because it does not come with visions, voices, or signs. It is a still settling of the Infinite into the soul's core—a **presence so vast it no longer announces itself**.

Hermetic Insight

"You shall not call Him; He shall come. And when He comes, He will say nothing, for He will be within."
(*CH XV*)

"When the temple is cleansed, the god enters—not by storm, but by stillness."
(*CH XIII*)

"The soul, once made fit, no longer travels—the divine takes up its dwelling and becomes the soul's breath." (*Asclepius*)

Implication

This law reveals the end of striving. Once the soul is fully opened, the Divine no longer stands above—it **becomes the inner atmosphere**. You do not rise endlessly—you are **inhabited eternally**. The One does not wait at the summit—it waits in the stillness that **only your surrender can unveil**.

This law is drawn from *Corpus Hermeticum XV, CH XIII,* and the *Asclepius*—particularly the doctrines on divine embodiment—where Hermes unveils a final and subtle truth: that the soul's ascent is mirrored by a **silent descent** of the Divine into the soul. In *CH XIII*, while guiding Tat through the final stages of rebirth, Hermes explains that the purified initiate does not simply rise toward the Divine—**the Divine also descends** into the soul, clothing itself in the inner temple prepared through discipline, purification, and gnosis. This descent is not dramatic, but **silent**—a still merging of essence with essence, where the Divine takes residence within the human without sound or spectacle.

In *CH XV*, Hermes speaks of a reversal hidden in the spiritual path: though we think we are moving toward God, it is in truth **God who is drawing near**—seeking entry into a soul that has made itself a fit vessel. In the *Asclepius*, this doctrine is affirmed in the teachings on divine embodiment, where the human being is described not just as a reflection of the Divine, but as a **habitation**—a sacred statue in whom the gods **choose to dwell**, when the form has been transfigured by inner light.

The Law of Silent Reversal teaches that the spiritual journey is not unidirectional. The soul rises, but only by surrendering, and as it surrenders, the Divine descends. This is the secret of true union: not the soul storming the gates of heaven, but heaven **gently inhabiting the soul**. The initiate who lives this law understands that enlightenment is not an attainment but a **welcoming**—a clearing of the inner space for the Presence to silently enter, dwell, and become one with the innermost "I." It is in this reversal that the mystery of the Two becoming One is fulfilled—**without a word, without movement, with only pure being remaining.**

LAW 43: THE LAW OF THE ETERNAL STRANGER (GOD AS THE UNKNOWN WITHIN)

Source: *Corpus Hermeticum VI, CH IX, Asclepius (meditations on divine unknowability)*

The Hermetica teaches that the Divine, though intimately present within all things, is **forever unknowable in its essence**. Even as the soul is united with the All, it finds that what it embraces is not a conclusion, but an **ever-deepening mystery**. God is both your innermost being and your **eternal stranger**—a presence that exceeds every concept, name, or image.

The highest knowledge is not certainty, but **reverent bewilderment**—a clarity that beholds the Unknown not as absence, but as the **overflow of absolute being**.

Hermetic Insight

"You seek to name the divine, but He who is within you cannot be spoken. He is the stranger dwelling in your innermost light."
(CH VI)

"I touched the fire, but it receded; I beheld the light, but it withdrew into itself. This is God—always near, always beyond."
(CH IX)

> "To know Him is to know that you do not know—and to rejoice that He remains greater than your knowing."
> (*Asclepius*)

Implication

This law invites you into **the mystery beyond all mastery**. The more you awaken, the more you will discover that the Divine is not a figure to capture—but a **living depth within you that never ceases to unfold**. The Eternal Stranger is not distant—it is **the divine within you, never reduced, never reached, but always known in love**.

This law is drawn from *Corpus Hermeticum VI, CH IX*, and the *Asclepius*, specifically the meditations on divine unknowability, where Hermes reveals that the Divine is not only the source of all being—it is also the **mystery at the heart of being**, forever known yet never fully grasped. In *CH VI*, Hermes teaches that the human soul carries within it the spark of the Divine, yet the closer one approaches it, the more it reveals itself as **infinite and unknowable**. This presence is **intimate**, dwelling in the very center of the self—yet it is also **alien**, always exceeding the mind's reach. It is the **Eternal Stranger**: the one within you that cannot be named.

In *CH IX*, Hermes emphasizes that divine wisdom begins with recognizing the limits of knowing. The soul may commune with God, but it cannot comprehend God as an object. The moment we try to define the Divine, we lose it. The *Asclepius* mirrors this teaching in its reverent reflections on divine mystery: God is that which gives all form but has **no form of its own**; that which animates all beings but remains **veiled**, even from the seer.

The Law of the Eternal Stranger teaches that the Divine is not merely distant—it is **inwardly transcendent**. It lives at the heart of consciousness as a **presence that cannot be domesticated**, a fire that burns but will not be held. To follow this law is to cultivate **awe without grasping**, intimacy without possession. The initiate who honors this truth walks with a paradox: the closer they draw to God, the more they surrender the need to know—and in that surrender, they touch the **face of the Unknown that lives within them**, loving, watching, and whispering from beyond the veil of self.

LAW 44: THE LAW OF RETURNLESS UNITY (THE END THAT HAS NO OPPOSITE)

Source: *Corpus Hermeticum XV, CH XIII, Silent fragmentary doctrines of the inner circle*

At the highest arc of Hermetic realization, the soul ceases not only to return—it ceases to reflect. There is no longer God *and* soul, light *and* knower, unity *and* awareness. All pairs, polarities, mirrors, and cycles dissolve. What remains is **pure Being, without a second**, without motion, without memory.

This is not union—it is **unicity**. Not communion—but **consummation**. The One absorbs its image, its emanation, its seeker—and what was once soul becomes **identity without distinction**. No return. No voice. No light reflecting light. **Only the Absolute, aware of itself as itself.**

Hermetic Insight

"He who becomes this One is not seen, for there is no other to see him. He is not named, for there is none to speak. He is not known, for there is no one left to know." (*CH XV*)

"Beyond the eighth, there is no voice, no motion, no ascent. There is the stillness that is all things before they were named."
(*CH XIII*)

"The soul dissolves its final veil, and there is no soul—only the One, returned to itself, not as homecoming, but as identity."
(*Hermetic fragment*)

Implication

This law is the true summit of Hermetic doctrine. It teaches that the **end is not reunion—it is the vanishing of all difference**. Beyond god and man, light and knower, self and cosmos, lies the unspoken finality: **Being as itself**, unreflected, unobserved, unconceived.

This law is drawn from *Corpus Hermeticum XV, CH XIII,* and the silent, fragmentary doctrines preserved within the **inner initiatory layers** of the Hermetic tradition, where Hermes imparts the most concealed mystery: the final state of the soul is not reunion—it is **unitary identity**. In *CH XIII*, as Hermes completes the rebirth of Tat, he unveils a truth that transcends even the cycles of return: the soul that has become God does not "go back" to the One—it **was never outside it**. The appearance of distance, of journey, of ascent and descent, dissolves in the radiance of **non-dual realization**. There is no longer self and God, knower and known—there is only **That Which Is**.

In the *silent fragments* passed on orally among the inner circle of initiates, it is said that this stage is not a destination, but a **consummation**—the dissolution of all opposites: above and below, motion and stillness, seeking and finding. The initiate who reaches this state does not experience return, for **there is nothing to return to**. Unity is not reunion. It is the end of all notions of departure. It is the awakening to **That Which Never Left**.

The Law of Returnless Unity teaches that the final truth is not transcendence of the world, nor immersion in it, but **the collapse of all distinctions**. The One is not beyond or within—it is **all that ever was, is, and will be**, without opposite, without boundary. The initiate who enters this state no longer says "I am one with God," for even that is too dualistic. They rest in the silence **before identity**, in the mystery **prior to the Word**, in a unity so total that **it has no direction, no contrast, and no return**. This is not the end of the journey. This is the **end of the idea of journey itself**.

Atlantean Scrolls Appendix

I. The Hidden Vessel Beneath the Guardian of Stone

(Inspired by Tablet XII — The Ship Beneath the Sphinx)

Beneath the lion that watches the ages, I sealed a vessel of light and memory.
Not for war, nor for fame, but for the hour when the stars tremble and man forgets.
Draw the line, sacred and true—from eye to apex, from stone to flame.
There shall the gate be found. Beneath, the key. Within, the fire.
Only those who carry the weightless heart shall pass into the chamber of awakening.
And when the dark tide rises once more, the vessel shall fly—not across the sky, but across the soul of man—bearing the Seed into the next dawn."

II. The Flame Within and the Masters of Time

(Inspired by Tablet X — The Key of Time)

There is a Flame hidden in your blood, waiting.
It does not burn with fire, but with remembrance.
Seven are the gates, and seven the tones.
As you pass through, your frequency will rise.
Know that the Lords of Time do not rule — they observe.
They wait for man to hear the music of his own becoming.
Align yourself, and the cycles will bend to your awakening.
Resist, and you will fall with the turning wheel, again and again."

III. THE HALLS OF THE HIDDEN SCROLLS

(*Inspired by Tablets II & VI — The Halls of Amenti & The Keys of Magic*)

Beneath the skin of the earth lie the scrolls not written with ink.
They are carved into the breath of the world, waiting for the silent ones.
There I walked with the Lords of Flame, in halls where time folds in on itself.
I placed the records of Atlantis—not to be read, but to be remembered.
When the soul is weighed and found worthy, these halls open inward, not downward.
They are not beneath the earth—they are beneath forgetting.
Enter, and you will find not knowledge—but yourself, before the world was born."

IV. THE SONG OF VIBRATION

(Inspired by Tablet X – The Key of Time)

Know that all is sound and all is motion,
The walls of the world are woven of tone.
He who masters vibration, moves without moving,
Walks through time as one walks through mist.
Each form is frozen music.
Each thought, a rhythm bound in light.
Speak, not with words, but with resonance.
Let your voice align the seven within you.
Then shall the gates open—not forward, but inward.
And time shall bend like reeds before the wind.

V. The Keepers of the Threshold

(Inspired by Tablets II and III)

In the chambers beneath the veil,
They stand: the Keepers of the Flame.
Neither gods nor men, they are the bridge.
Ancient beyond reckoning, still as stone,
They watch for the awakening of the few.
None may pass who carries weight in the heart.
None may enter with divided soul.
They ask no questions. They judge no creed.
Only light answers light.
Only truth can open the seal.

VI. THE DARK BROTHERS WHO FEED ON FEAR

(Inspired by Tablet VIII – The Key of Mystery)

Beware the ones who walk in shadow.
They do not dwell in night, but in deception.
They wear faces of wisdom but speak without flame.
They come in silence, feeding on fear.
Not of earth, yet bound to it.
Not mortal, yet they die with every lie.
You will know them by the chill they bring,
By the emptiness that follows their touch.
Shine your light—they will vanish like mist.
But should you waver, they shall plant seeds of sleep.

Protect your gate. Guard your thought.
For every careless word gives them a door.

VII. The Halls of Amenti

(Inspired by Tablet II – The Halls of Amenti)

Beneath the skin of the earth lies a door.
Not made of stone, but of silence.
Enter not with feet, but with stillness.
I descended there in the First Time,
Through fire, through shadow, through soundless gates.
Seven are the Lords who guard the passage,
Each with eyes like suns, unmoved by plea.
I lay myself down in the chamber of sleep,
Yet I did not sleep—I waited.
There I learned that death is illusion.
That time is the robe the soul sheds like dust.

Return there not by digging, but by remembering.
The Halls are within. The Light is within.
And those who find it shall live without end.

VIII. THE LORDS OF THE CYCLES

(Inspired by Tablet XII – Key of Prophecy)

Nine are the watchers, hidden in turning,
Holding the spiral of becoming in place.
Each moves in silence, older than stars,
Yet not one breathes without harmony.
They are not masters, but mirrors of Law.
They bend not the path—they hold it steady.
To them I gave account of my journey.
And they, in stillness, revealed the map.
All things move. All things return.
But the awakened do not revolve—they rise.

When the wheel breaks, the ones who remember
Shall walk straight through the center.

IX. The Light That Burns in the Shadow

(Inspired by Tablet VIII – The Key of Mystery)

Light there is that darkness cannot touch.
Not the sun, nor the flame, but the inward fire.
It speaks in silence. It shines through the bones.
The more it is hidden, the more it is whole.
I found it beneath the root of breath,
Where no thought stirs, where no name remains.
And when I looked upon it, it looked back.
Not with eyes, but with truth.
This is the Light before the gods.
This is the seed of your return.
Protect it, and it shall protect you.
Forget it, and the world becomes shadow.

But the flame still burns—even in sleep.

X. The Keys of Magic

(Inspired by Tablet VI – The Key of Magic)

Not all power is seen.
Not all movement makes sound.
Magic is the art of alignment —
The act of placing thought within the current of Law.
Speak not with force, but with precision.
Let your word carry harmony.
The world responds not to desire, but to resonance.

Guard the gate of your voice.
Let no vibration leave that does not serve the Flame.
For each word is a summons.
Each gesture a signature upon the unseen.

XI. THE PATH OF THE SERPENT FIRE

(Inspired by Tablet XV – Secret of Secrets)

Within your spine sleeps the Serpent,
Twined in rings, dreaming of stars.
Awaken it not with haste, but with reverence.
For the fire rises only when the vessel is ready.
Seven are the gates it must pierce,
Seven the seals upon your soul.
When opened in order, they birth the Light.
When torn open, they unleash the storm.

The fire is not yours.
It is the Divine remembering itself in you.

XII. The Sun Behind the Sun

(Inspired by Tablet IV – The Space Born)

There is a light behind all lights,
A sun that no eye has seen.
It is not above, but within.
I have seen it, and I have become it.
It shines through stars, yet needs no flame.
This is the true center—the womb of all radiance.
From it I came, and to it I return.
Not by death, but by remembrance.

Seek not the heavens.
Seek the light that makes heavens possible.

XIII. The Silence Before the Word

(*Inspired by Tablet VII – The Seven Lords*)

Before the Word, there was Silence—
Not absence, but presence unspoken.
From that stillness came the pulse,
And from the pulse, the breath of being.
The Word was formed, not from sound,
But from the will to remember.

Seven were they who stood in the beginning,
Silent Lords beyond time and flame.
Each a ray, each a law, each a keeper of balance.
They did not speak, but through them the Law was uttered.
Through them came motion, form, and the scaffolding of worlds.

Lord of Flame,
Lord of Form,
Lord of Time,
Lord of Space,
Lord of Matter,

Lord of Motion,
Lord of Light.

These are the pillars beneath creation,
The thoughts before thought, the tones beneath all music.
You do not see them—you are shaped by them.
They do not speak, yet all truth comes through their silence.

Return to that silence often.
For there, the Word shall be born again in you.
And you shall remember—not just who you are,
But what sustains the All.

XIV. The Death That Is Not Death

(Inspired by Tablet III – The Key of Wisdom)

I laid my body in stone.
I watched it sleep as I wandered the stars.
Death is not what men believe.
It is not an end, but a door.
The body fades, but the Flame remains.
The self dissolves, but the Light persists.
Know that you are not the shell,
But the motion within it.
And when the moment comes,
You will shed your skin and walk unbound.

To die is to wake, if you have remembered.

XV. My Departure and Return

(Inspired by Tablet XIII – The Keys of Life and Death)

I go now beyond the veil,
Not to abandon, but to await the appointed hour.
When man has risen once more,
When the Flame burns clean again,
I shall return—not in body, but in mind.
Not in word, but in light.

Guard well these teachings.
They are keys, not creeds.
And when the darkness returns,
Let them become the stars that guide you.

I am not gone.
I have only changed my shape.

Thoth I was. Light I remain.

Final Prophecy of Thoth

The Hidden Vessel Beneath the Guardian of Stone

"I speak to the ones not yet born, to those whose inner flame has not been extinguished. In the First Time, I descended and carved my secrets in stone and silence. Beneath the guardian beast with the face of man and the form of lion, I placed a vessel—not of this world, nor of this age."

"This craft, of fire and resonance, I sealed in the land of Khem, that it might sleep through the ages. It shall not rise until the stars are shaken and the dark ones return from the deep void."

"To the wise: trace a line from the eye of the watcher to the crown of the sacred peak. Mark another in perfect accord. There you will find the passage, veiled in stone and shadow, leading to what I have hidden."

"Beneath the gate, beneath the temple, beneath the memory of mankind—it waits. Not only a ship, but a mirror of time. And near it, the scrolls of flame—the records of the first world, sealed before the birth of flesh."

"I give no key but this: only the heart aligned with the Seven shall see. Only the soul that has weighed itself in the light shall pass. For what is hidden shall not awaken for power—but for remembrance. And when the darkness falls again, and men no longer remember their origin, then shall the fire rise once more. And those who ride the vessel shall become the seed of the next dawn."

METAPHYSICAL COMMENTARY: THE SEAL BENEATH THE SPHINX

The **ship** Thoth speaks of is not merely a physical vessel—it is a symbol of divine memory, cosmic technology, and **transcendent motion across time and dimension**. Hidden beneath the Sphinx—a guardian of mystery—this vessel is bound not just by stone, but by spiritual law. It can only be awakened when consciousness itself has reached the required resonance.

The **"line drawn from the image to the apex"** refers to sacred geometry, a map encoded into the land by Thoth himself. The intersection of these lines is a **gateway between worlds**, both literal and vibrational.

The **Halls of Records**, though not named directly, are referenced as the place where **thought has been crystallized**—a realm beneath matter where the history of Atlantis and humanity is stored in energetic form. These are the **Halls of Amenti**, accessed not only by excavation but by **initiation**.

The **return of darkness** is not merely political or social—it is the **re-emergence of collective amnesia**, the loss of divine identity. The return of the Light, therefore, must begin within the soul of the awakened. The **ship**, then, is a metaphor for the **vehicle of higher consciousness**, which those initiated into the Flame will ride—across destruction, into the new cycle.

This final law, unspoken among the 44, is the seal of them all:
The return is already encoded.
The ship is already within you.
The gate is memory, and the key is alignment.
When darkness forgets, the Light shall remember.

www.ingramcontent.com/pod-product-compliance
Lightning Source LLC
Chambersburg PA
CBHW051615230426
43668CB00013B/2113